Prereading Activities for Content Area Reading and Learning

Third Edition

John E. Readence
University of Nevada, Las Vegas
Las Vegas, Nevada, USA

David W. Moore
Arizona State University West
Phoenix, Arizona, USA

Robert J. Rickelman
University of North Carolina–
Charlotte
Charlotte, North Carolina, USA

INTERNATIONAL
Reading
Association

800 Barksdale Road, PO Box 8139
Newark, Delaware 19714-8139, USA
www.reading.org

The International Reading Association attempts, through its publications, to provide a forum for a wide spectrum of opinions on reading. This policy permits divergent viewpoints without implying the endorsement of the Association.

Director of Publications   Joan M. Irwin
Editor in Chief, Books   Matthew W. Baker
Permissions Editor   Janet S. Parrack
Associate Editor   Tori Mello
Publications Coordinator   Beth Doughty
Association Editor   David K. Roberts
Production Department Manager   Iona Sauscermen
Art Director   Boni Nash
Senior Electronic Publishing Specialist   Anette Schütz-Ruff
Electronic Publishing Specialist   Cheryl J. Strum
Electronic Publishing Assistant   Jeanine K. McGann

Project Editor   Matthew W. Baker

Library of Congress Cataloging-in-Publication Data
Readence, John E., 1947–
   Prereading activities for content area reading and learning / John E. Readence, David W. Moore, Robert J. Rickelman.—3rd ed.
      p.   cm.
   Moore's name appears first on the earlier edition.
   Includes bibliographical references and index.
   1. Reading readiness.   2. Content area reading.   I. Moore, David W.   II. Rickelman, Robert J.   III. Title.
LB1050.43.M66   2000   00-028140
428.4'07—dc21
0-87207-261-4

Fourth Printing, August 2004

Contents

Preface

Prereading Activities for Content Area Reading and Learning, third edition, is similar to the first and second editions in that it describes numerous ways to prepare middle and secondary school students to learn from printed materials. It is a collection of strategies that teachers and students can employ, and we provide examples along with descriptions of each activity. The activities are grounded on the principle that prereading preparation is essential for maximum learning.

This third edition differs from the second edition in two significant ways. First, the second edition was written more than a decade ago. Much new material has been uncovered in the research and practice of prereading activities since that time. Therefore, each of the first six chapters of the third edition has been revised and updated to reflect this wealth of new information. Second, we conclude this edition with a new chapter on combining prereading activities. Adding this chapter allows us to suggest ways in which prereading activities discussed throughout the book may be used in concert with one another, whether in lesson-based or unit-based planning and teaching. Additionally, it allows us to come full circle by connecting these teaching suggestions to the concepts presented in the introductory chapter. As with the first and second editions, this book is meant to be a practical guide to activities that are intended to promote the learning of adolescents in the day-to-day milieu of content classrooms. It is our hope that you find this book helpful in your teaching.

JER
DWM
RJR

Chapter 1

Preparing Students to Read in the Content Areas

PURPOSE

Chapter 1 sets the stage for this book by presenting what teachers should consider when preparing students to read in content areas. This chapter opens with a brief introduction to instructional scaffolding, then describes segments of instruction educators should take into account when planning to teach. Next, it addresses cycles of instruction. The chapter ends with a description of factors that affect learning.

Content areas such as biology, history, and vocational arts present distinctive viewpoints and explanations of the world. Reading materials used during the study of these subjects often contain unfamiliar concepts, strange terms, and unusual styles of writing. Consequently, students require scaffolding.

Scaffolding means supporting students before, during, and after they read. It is a process of enabling students to accomplish what is normally beyond their abilities. Scaffolding means providing enough help so students can succeed with a task that otherwise would be impossible (Graves & Graves, 1994).

Prereading scaffolding means that teachers perform activities such as relating passage contents to students' worlds, presenting key vocabulary prior to encountering it in text, and noting the organization of a passage so students can use it as a tool for understanding. Teachers also introduce students to general ideas they will encounter, and they encourage an active search for meaning. Some of the talk that typically occurs after reading is moved to before the reading begins. Prereading scaffolding is the opposite of simply handing out challenging text passages and expecting students to learn.

The value of preparing students for reading has been recognized in professional literature since the turn of the 20th century (see, for example, De Garmo, 1896; McMurray, 1909). Research continues to support the practice of preparing students for reading and learning. For instance, Alexander and Jetton (2000) report that students seeking to learn from unfamiliar documents "require clear scaffolding that aids them in building a meaningful base of content knowledge and the seeds of personal interest."

Planning effective prereading activities for content area reading and learning is complicated. Our presentation of the considerations to be made during such planning begins with time frames that teachers commonly address.

Instructional Time Frames

Instructional planning in the classroom generally is broken down according to segments of time. Yearly, unit, and lesson considerations are three common time frames.

Yearly Time Frame

Planning for the school year often includes articulating a vision, then deciding where you intend to lead class members and how you will share those intentions. Vision statements for reading and learning might be expressed like a goal (To become independent lifelong learners) or a slogan (Reading gives us power!). Posting the statement(s) helps guide everyday decision making and reflecting by you and your students.

Yearly plans also involve time lines for the formal curriculum. More and more states are requiring students to achieve specific standards (e.g., Students will compare and contrast information), so educators are planning when and how they intend to directly address curriculum requirements during the academic year. When considering these requirements, educators also plan long-term series of instructional activities that connect their actions. For instance, teachers may plan to develop students' compare and contrast proficiencies by designing a coherent focus on these skills throughout the year.

A common prereading practice conducted at the beginning of each school year or term that has implications for the entire year involves introductions to assigned reading materials. Many teachers conduct a discussion on how to use text features such as tables of contents, glossaries, and chapter headings (Gee & Rakow, 1991). A student-directed way to approach this practice is through text surveys (Huffman, 1996). Teachers introduce a text as if it were a new class member, noting why it is joining this class and giving some general background on it. Students generate a list of questions and then survey the text to find what is in it for them. Next, they conduct a whole-class follow-up to address what features they found and to talk about how to best treat them. If practice exercises are included, then students plan for their use; if no glossary is available, then the class might decide to construct their own.

Unit Time Frame

Units are a middle level of instructional planning that encompass blocks of time lasting from a few days to a few weeks. Units of instruction embed teaching-learning processes around organizing centers such as a(n)

- genre (poetry, short story),
- issue (What should be done about pollution?),
- novel (*Roll of Thunder, Hear My Cry, The Fallen Angels*),
- theme (identity, patterns), and
- topic (solar system, colonial America).

Units that pose central questions about their organizing centers go far in emphasizing productive reading and thinking (Wiggins & McTighe, 1998). Central questions define students as problem solvers addressing multilayered and provocative concerns that cannot be answered in a single sentence. The questions engage students with course contents, allowing multiple responses at different levels of sophistication. The following queries exemplify central questions:

- What is a hero?
- Who is a friend?
- Why is the weather difficult to predict?
- What most influences healthy human development?
- In which decade of the 1900s were Americans better off?
- What are appropriate limits to freedom of speech?

Working backward, or designing down, from central questions (e.g, What is a hero?) and from curriculum standards (e.g., Students will compare and contrast information) leads to appropriate prereading scaffolding (Erickson, 1998). For instance, students addressing the question, What is a hero?, along with compare/contrast would require scaffolds such as appropriate introductions, clear expectations, accessible print and nonprint resources, guidelines for expressing themselves, and lessons on how to accomplish specific tasks. Additionally, if students were to learn what a hero is as well as how to compare and contrast information, then prereading, during reading, and postreading activities should work in concert with these expectations. Although this book emphasizes activities before students read, review and enrichment during and after reading clearly deserve attention.

Lesson Time Frame

Lessons are teaching events that focus on definite learning tasks. They concentrate on the specific tasks that enable students to accomplish general expectations. After conducting a task analysis of a unit's central question, consulting curriculum standards, and thinking about students' competencies, educators might see the need for several lessons to provide appropriate scaffolding. In a unit on heroism, teachers might decide to teach a lesson on gathering information (e.g., accessing Internet sites, library materials, and personal interviews). They might see the need for a lesson on assigning adjectives (e.g., *crafty, resolute, dignified*) that characterize literary and real-life people.

Another lesson derived from a heroism unit might be on comparing and contrasting characters. In this lesson, educators might plan to teach students how to use a Data Chart such as the following:

Character	Situations Encountered	Actions Performed	Personal Characteristics
Mahatma Gandhi			
Eleanor Roosevelt			
Superman			

If students are to produce an explanation of heroism, then additional lessons might be included on making sense of the information (determining supportable similarities among Mahatma Gandhi, Eleanor Roosevelt, and Superman) and expressing themselves (constructing a poster presentation).

In brief, thinking of instruction according to yearly, unit, and lesson time frames helps manage instructional planning. These time segments provide structure to a complicated aspect of teaching.

Instructional Cycles

Within yearly, unit, and lesson time frames, educators plan cycles of instruction. These cycles are recurring series of teaching-learning events that turn back on themselves. They have many labels and descriptions, although they most frequently are said to consist of three overlapping events. We call these cyclical events of instruction *demonstration, guided practice*, and *independent application*, terms from past research on direct instruction (Rosenshine & Stevens, 1986).

Teachers begin the demonstration stage as the dominant figure in the class; then they begin fading out their role so students become the dominant figures as they independently apply what has been taught. Demonstration calls for teachers to explain a concept (such as heroism) or model a learning strategy (such as completing a Data Chart). During this event teachers also attempt to engage students in learning by demonstrating a topic's relevance and arousing curiosity.

The guided practice event in the instructional cycle involves inquiry, exercises, feedback, and possible reteaching. For instance, after demonstrating how to construct a Data Chart, students read and complete their own. Having students explain their performance to others helps clarify the strategy. After charts are completed, students might compare their work with that of the teacher's or other students. Frequent opportunities to utilize charts and receive feedback should be offered during this stage.

Independent application is meant to help students integrate into their repertoires what is being taught. Demonstration and guided practice sessions lead to successful independent applications. For instance, allow class time for students to apply Data Charts in their own study. Plan culminating activities based on charted information, and encourage students to use their charts during quizzes and tests. Record a weekly grade for students who chart particular passages. The goal of these independent application activities is to provide relevant situations for students to use what has been presented.

In brief, instruction involves cycles. Teachers take the lead during demonstrations, teachers and students provide equal input during guided practice, and students dominate during independent application. Teachers fade out and students fade in during these cycles. These cyclical events help mark beginnings, middles, and endings within units and lessons.

Factors That Affect Learning

When planning cycles of instruction within certain time frames, educators account for factors that affect learning from text. *Expected learning outcomes, motivation and engagement, content knowledge, attention,* and *learning strategies* are five key factors. Teachers can manipulate these factors to scaffold students' learning about the world, and students can manipulate them independently. If appropriate learning outcomes are made known, if students are motivated and engaged with their learning, if their content knowledge is sufficient, if they know what information deserves attention, and if they apply appropriate strategies, then learning from text can be expected. The remainder of this chapter explains how each factor affects learning from text and suggests how prereading activities promote these factors.

Expected Learning Outcomes

Outcomes are what students are expected to acquire or develop during their study of a particular subject. Determining expected learning outcomes often begins with consulting relevant curriculum documents; matching content standards (Describe functions of the executive branch of the U.S. government) with reading standards (Identify important information) guides instructional planning.

Expected learning outcomes help define classroom efforts that are acceptable. Teachers and students who examine scoring guides, or rubrics, and who scan examples of what to produce go far in clarifying expectations and promoting learning. Knowing the indicators of satisfactory learning enhances efforts to accomplish the learning.

A difficulty in matching content and reading standards is that content area specialists often believe information is stated directly in a text when, in fact, it is only mentioned indirectly. This occurs because content area teachers know their discipline so well that the mere mention of a concept triggers their knowledge of the concept. Unfortunately, mention of a concept might trigger practically nothing in students' minds. For instance, a science text might mention that Darwin's theory of evolution changed people's view of the world as fundamentally as did Copernicus's theory of the solar system. This information might convey to a specialist a clear perspective on Darwin, but expecting students to understand it might be unreasonable. Given the relative value of information for different people, teachers need to read materials with a student's perspective to determine what prereading preparation students will require.

Helping students realize the expected outcomes of instruction is a valuable type of instructional scaffold. Considering the clarity with which texts present particular information informs instructional decisions about prereading preparation.

Motivation and Engagement

Along with expected learning outcomes, the motivation readers have relative to reading influences learning. Some reading materials engage readers by the nature of topics presented or with devices such as visuals, problems to be solved, and anecdotes that connect information with students' lives. These materials build on the preexisting motivations of students. Other materials provide lifeless information. Additionally, some students are highly motivated, eager learners with the urge to master new information, whereas others are marginalized, frustrated, and view reading assignments as something to avoid. Before leading students through content materials, teachers frequently need to engage students in the journey. Students who will not read are as disadvantaged as students who cannot read.

Effectively motivating and engaging students in reading and learning can be accomplished many ways (see Guthrie & Wigfield, 2000). Teachers provide clear feedback and earned praise, and they maintain a positive outlook. They promote self-directed learning and provide choices of materials to read and tasks to perform. They connect course content (e.g., amphibians) with real-world interactions (e.g., live frogs and salamanders in the classroom).

Teachers promote social participation and collaboration to motivate and engage readers. They do this by offering inquiry approaches that encompass a range of texts (Bean, 2000; Wade & Moje, 2000). For instance, students discuss literature in peer-led groups, respond to what they read through cooperative productions such as skits and role plays, and jointly investigate real-world problems such as pollution. Students come together with community members through activities such as guest presentations, visits to local sites, personal interviews, and project partnerships.

Teachers also stimulate curiosity because they realize that it determines much motivation and engagement. Young children, adolescents, and adults want to explore their environments. When presented with a new stimulus, people want to know about it. This natural phenomenon drives people to seek information. Capitalizing on students' curiosity is a motivational strategy that can be addressed readily during prereading activities.

Content Knowledge

Assuming that learning outcomes are accepted and students are motivated to read, successful learning depends largely on students' prior knowledge of the content. Two important aspects of this are amount of knowledge and activation of knowledge.

Amount of knowledge. Already knowing a lot about what is on a page promotes learning. To appreciate this point, read the following paragraph and retell it in your own words:

> Two experiments investigated visual processing asymmetries in normal and dyslexic readers, with unilateral tachistoscopic presentations. The experiments employed randomized or blocked presentations of verbal and nonverbal materials to determine whether previously reported differences between dyslexics and normals were due to structural hemispheric differences or to strategical processing differences. The results indicate that if dyslexics are unable to predict the nature of the stimulus, they behave as normal readers. Their atypical laterality emerges only when they can adopt a strategy in anticipation of a specific type of stimulus. (Underwood & Boot, 1986, p. 219)

Could you retell this passage in your own words? You probably were motivated enough to read it carefully, and you knew the expected outcome, but your learning was most likely incomplete due to limited content knowledge.

In order to understand the sample paragraph, prior knowledge is needed about visual processing asymmetries, unilateral tachistoscopic presentations, and randomized or blocked presentations. You need to know these specific terms and have a general idea about the type of research being conducted. If you did not know much about what the paragraph reported, your learning was impaired.

Some materials present concepts that are more familiar than others. Some science books present *erosion* and *tides*; others present *heliozoans* and *interoceptors*. The differences in clarity of presentation also can be surprising. Well-written materials explain ideas various ways. If *condensation* were to be introduced, a well-written science text would define it by stating that in condensation a gas or vapor loses heat, decreases in volume, and turns into a solid or liquid. The text would illustrate products of condensation such as clouds, rain, snow, frost, and sweat on glasses of ice water. *Condensation* might be contrasted with *evaporation*, and the base word, *dense*, might be highlighted. The natural tendency for matter to contract when it becomes cold could be stated. Conversely, a poorly written text might introduce condensation by stating cryptically that it involves uniting molecules to form new, heavier, and more complex compounds.

In order to plan effective content reading lessons, examine the familiarity of the passage contents, and determine the amount of content knowledge students require in order to achieve expected learning outcomes. The gap between what your students already know and what passages present helps determine what teachers need to provide during the prereading stage of an assignment.

Activation of knowledge. For maximum learning, students need prior knowledge about the topic being studied and they need to relate that prior knowledge to the contents of the passage. To appreciate this point, read the following:

> The procedure is actually quite simple. First you arrange items into different groups. Of course one pile may be sufficient depending on how much there is to do. If you have to go somewhere else due to lack of facilities that is the next step; otherwise, you are pretty well set. It is important not to overdo things. That is, it is better to do too few things at once than too many. In the short run this may not seem important but complications can easily arise. A mistake can be expensive as well. At first, the whole procedure will seem complicated. Soon, however, it will become just another facet of life. It is difficult to foresee any end to the necessity for this task in the immediate future, but then, one never can tell. After the procedure is completed one arranges the materials into different groups again. Then they can be put into their appropriate places. Eventually they will be used once more and the whole cycle will then have to be repeated. However, that is part of life. (Bransford & Johnson, 1972, p. 722)

You may have thought this paragraph was incomprehensible. Individual sentences made sense, but the paragraph did not seem to hang together. If you were to retell everything you could remember about the paragraph, your recall score probably would be quite low. However, if you had known before reading the passage that it was about washing clothes, you would have thought it comprehensible.

As demonstrated, knowing about the contents of a passage is important, but such knowledge is useless if it is not related to the contents of the passage being studied. Knowing something about washing clothes is important for understanding the sample paragraph; knowing that the passage is about washing clothes is equally important.

It is important to realize that the activities included in this book focus more on *activating* prior knowledge than on *developing* it. These activities involve oral or pencil and paper tasks; they help activate what students already know. Additional teaching probably will be needed if students have little knowledge of the subject. Direct experiences with concrete objects, pictures, films, guest speakers, experiments, and field trips might be needed in order to develop students' content knowledge.

Attention

Learners have a limited capacity for absorbing and making sense of information. This becomes readily apparent when two people talk to you at the same time. You must internally turn off one message and listen only to the other or you will be overwhelmed and miss both messages. Because of limited capacities, readers need to attend to the important information in a passage and disregard what is trivial. Otherwise, all words, phrases, sentences, and paragraphs appear worth learning, and the barrage of information is overwhelming. Efficient readers direct their attention to the important ideas. Focusing attention deserves time during prereading activities along with clarifying expected learning outcomes, motivating students, and developing and activating content knowledge.

The reader or the writer can determine what deserves attention. Readers' purposes for reading and writers' presentations of information regulate readers' attention (van Dijk, 1979). To illustrate, think of skimming a history text for a particular date to use in a report. The writer might have mentioned the date only one time because it was considered to be of minor importance, but the reader might consider the date to be the crucial aspect of the passage. For another example, read the following paragraph:

Native Americans

The biggest differences that developed among the Native Americans were a result of where they settled to live. There were five main living centers where these people settled: the Northwest Coast, the California region, the Southwest, the Eastern woodlands, and the Plains.

Some readers might decide that the important information in the paragraph is what caused the biggest differences among Native Americans; others might think the number of main living centers deserves emphasis; still others might focus on locations of living centers. Moreover, one might read only to determine if the Southeast were considered a main living center of Native Americans, and another might study the passage to determine if it is well written. All five or none of these purposes could constitute acceptable reasons for reading. Readers' purposes for reading influence the aspects of a passage that deserve attention.

Although readers frequently let their specific reasons for reading regulate their attention, they also allow writers to regulate their attention. Rather than search for specific information, readers often study a passage to learn what the author emphasized and thus considered important.

Writers accentuate important information several ways, and textbook writers rely quite heavily on adjunct aids. Adjunct aids consist of parts of texts such as the questions and activities inserted in a chapter; typography such as boldfaced headings, subheadings, and marked words; pictorial aids such as pictures, illustrations, diagrams, maps, tables, and graphs; glossaries and footnotes; and introductions and summaries. These pieces of text are adjunct because they either highlight or complete the meaning of the main body of the text. They are designed to lead readers to important information.

Many current textbooks contain adjunct aids. The questions and activities encourage students to go beyond the information given in the text, and the pictorial aids supplement textual information. Teachers should examine these aids to see whether the writer emphasized information that fits their curriculum.

Attention affects what is learned from text. During the prereading stage of reading lessons, teachers decide whether they should help students focus their attention on pertinent information or have students focus without help. In addition, teachers and students decide whether the students' purposes for reading or the writer's presentation of ideas should direct attention.

Learning Strategies

Learning outcomes can be clarified during a lesson. Students might have appropriate levels of motivation, their content knowledge might be sufficient and active, and their attention might be directed to information, but they still could have difficulty understanding and remembering text information because of their learning strategies.

Learning strategies are tactics employed to achieve certain goals. Many strategies have been identified through the years (see, for example, Kucan & Beck, 1997; Laycock & Russell, 1941; Weinstein & Mayer, 1986), a few of which are visualizing information, rereading troublesome parts of a passage, reviewing information frequently, and creating mnemonic devices. Three powerful strategies that can be incorporated readily into prereading lessons are *predicting, connecting,* and *organizing* (Moore, Moore, Cunningham, & Cunningham, 1998).

Predicting. Predicting involves anticipating the information in a passage and calls for readers to think ahead while reading. Once readers have a set of expectations for a passage, they can read and see which expectations are met, which are not, and what unexpected information is encountered. Students who do not predict upcoming information generally are unprepared for the stream of ideas they encounter.

Helping students predict information is an essential feature of the prereading teaching strategies presented in the remaining chapters of this book. ReQuest, PReP, Contextual Redefinition, Webbing, and Free Writing all provide students an advance idea of the contents of upcoming passages. These teaching strategies help students predict the contents of passages written about diverse topics. In addition, they can be converted to learning strategies by having students assume responsibility for previewing passages and forming predictions.

Connecting. Perhaps the best way to learn new information is to connect it to prior knowledge. Connecting involves relating what is being presented to what is already known; linking new information to old is the essence of the connect learning strategy. To illustrate, think back to the passage on Native Americans earlier in this chapter. You might connect the information in that passage with what you already know by thinking of specific tribes in the five main living centers: "I know about the Apache, Navajo, and Pueblo Indians in the Southwest, and I know their traditional way of life differs from the Sioux and Comanche Indians of the Plains." Remembering the principle that environment influences life helps explain why differences are found among American Indians.

Connecting information enhances learning. New concepts are fitted into a network of preexisting concepts, thereby holding the information in place and providing access to it. Teaching strategies that promote prediction also promote connections. For instance, Webbing and Free Writing encourage students to assimilate new information with the old. (See Chapters 5 and 6 for more information on these strategies.)

Organizing. Organizing information is another powerful learning strategy. Students who arrange ideas according to meaningful classifications have an advantage over those who do not. Part of organizing information involves following the pattern of ideas presented by an author. Readers who are sensitive to an author's writing patterns typically learn more than readers who are insensitive to the patterns. Thus, it seems worthwhile to help students determine whether passages are written according to a pattern such as time sequence, simple listing, or problem solution. The Survey Technique and Data Charts presented in this book are prereading strategies that emphasize the organization of passages (see Chapters 2 and 6).

Another part of organizing information involves assimilating ideas according to readers' prior knowledge. This aspect of organizing is quite similar to connecting information. To illustrate, animal life can be studied according to body systems such as respiration, musculature, and reproduction. Once students know the organization of body systems, that structure can be used when studying new life forms. Students could organize information about any animal's body system regardless of the writer's presentation. In a sense, students' minds have a set of labeled slots to fill. Webbing and Graphic Organizing are two strategies that capitalize on organizing information according to students' prior knowledge (see Chapter 5).

Summary

This chapter introduced the idea of instructional scaffolding, then presented three segments of time that provide structure to planning instructional scaffolds: yearly, unit, and lesson time frames. Instructional cycles consisting of three events—demonstration, guided practice, and independent application—mark the beginning, middle, and end of units and lessons.

The final section of the chapter described five factors that affect learning from text: expected learning outcomes, motivation and engagement, content knowledge, attention, and learning strategies. It is important to realize that all five factors can be addressed during the prereading stage of units and lessons to promote learning from text. Throughout the school year or term students can be taught to manipulate these factors independently.

Chapter 2

Asking and Answering Questions Before Reading

PURPOSE

This chapter demonstrates the effective use of questions to guide students' learning and prescribes a set of teaching and learning strategies designed to allow students to assume responsibility for asking their own questions of texts in independent learning situations.

Strategies

1. *Question-Answer Relationships* (QAR) is an activity that helps students answer comprehension questions more efficiently by analyzing the task demands of various types of questions.

2. The *Directed Reading Activity* (DRA) uses teacher questions to activate prior knowledge, create interest, and establish purposes for reading.

3. The *Scaffolded Reading Experience* (SRE) is another, more eclectic strategy that uses teacher questions as the basis for the pre-reading engagement of students with text.

4. The *ReQuest* procedure helps students formulate their own questions about the text they are reading and develop effective questioning behaviors.

5. The *Directed Reading-Thinking Activity* (DRTA) provides guided practice for students in setting their own purposes for reading.

6. The *Survey Technique* helps students preview a text and independently formulate their own purposes for reading.

Questions play an integral part in learning about the world. It is difficult to imagine attempting to function effectively without asking questions and receiving answers. Questions also play a dominant role in reading and learning from text, and they are a major tool in the instructional repertoire of teachers.

The questioning strategies included here are designed to stimulate students' curiosity about a passage to be read, activate prior content knowledge, lead students to anticipate and elaborate on what they read, and focus attention on important information. The expected learning outcome is that students will use questions to set their own purposes for reading text material. In addition, the strategies to be discussed demonstrate a progression from teacher demonstration and modeling of effective questioning (using the DRA and SRE), to student guided practice in using effective questioning (using ReQuest and DRTA), to independent student questioning (using the Survey Technique). This progression is intended to lead students from dependent to independent learning from text.

Levels of Processing

Before proceeding to a discussion of specific teaching strategies, one important aspect of questioning should be considered: the level of understanding of the text by students. Pearson and Johnson (1978) provide a framework for developing questions that help students use their own thoughts and prior experiences to interact with the information in a text. The levels of processing construct is a tool to help teachers lead students beyond merely imitating an author's words.

Pearson and Johnson proposed three levels of text processing: text explicit, text implicit, and script implicit or experience-based. Text explicit processing involves getting the facts as stated in a text. A text explicit question is cued explicitly by the language of the text. Readers can point to the answer in the text, and there is only one correct answer. Text implicit processing, on the other hand, requires readers to determine an appropriate answer drawn from the text and from their prior knowledge. Text implicit questions are based on the language of the text but require readers to derive an answer not directly visible in the text. Readers are asked to infer what the text implicitly states and elaborate on the given information. Readers take the facts presented in the text and add their own prior knowledge to derive a plausible answer implied by the author. Answers may vary depending on the type of experiences readers bring to the text but must be consistent with the information stated. Finally, experience-based processing requires readers to think beyond what is stated in the text. When experience-based questions are asked, readers must draw information from their prior knowledge to derive plausible answers. Answers to these questions are based mainly on reader experience as they are not obtained directly from the text, making possible numerous answers. The following paragraph with accompanying questions illustrates these levels of processing:

The Quest

As Tom peered through the thick undergrowth, he could barely make out the figure that stared back at him. Cautious not to let the heat of the sun confuse his judgment, he trudged closer to the figure to identify it more accurately.

1. What was Tom peering through?

2. Where was Tom?

3. What else might Tom have done after seeing the figure?

In question 1, the answer comes directly from the text—*thick undergrowth*. In question 2, the answer is not directly visible. Thus, the facts of *thick undergrowth*, *heat of the sun*, and *trudged* might be added with prior knowledge to answer *jungle*, *woods*, or *savanna*. All these answers are plausible interpretations given the language of the text and the different backgrounds of readers. Finally, in question 3, many answers would be allowable as they are not derived from the text but from readers' experiences.

Teacher Questioning

There are a number of considerations about teacher-originated questions to keep in mind in order to enhance students' reading and learning. First, formulating good questions representative of all levels of processing requires time and thought. Second, questions must provide specific cues for students' comprehension. General, diffuse questions might not facilitate comprehension; questions should provide the cues needed for students to respond. Third, what you ask about is what students learn. For example, students who read to find answers stated explicitly in a text tend to learn only that information. This technique may be helpful when the text is especially dense. On the other hand, students who read to answer higher level questions that call for text implicit or experience-based processing tend to acquire more overall information from a text.

Finally, students who have learned to depend on teachers to ask questions may not learn to ask appropriate questions of themselves. We must remember that students are conditioned to respond rather than to initiate. Teacher questions (1) are not necessarily the questions students would ask or want to have answered, (2) crowd out students' opportunities to ask questions, and (3) do not permit teachers to find out whether students are learning to ask questions on their own. In other words, answering questions only indirectly teaches the skills necessary for independent reading.

Question-Answer Relationships

Students should be proficient in answering questions before we ask them to generate their own. The Question-Answer Relationships (QAR) strategy (Raphael, 1984, 1986) can help students learn to answer questions appropriately.

QARs help students identify responses to questions. Using Pearson and Johnson's (1978) levels of processing construct, Raphael suggested teaching students to use the three processing levels, relabeled for ease of understanding. Her terminology for the three levels and the mnemonics used for each are: *right there* (text explicit)—words used to create the question and words used for the answer are in the same sentence; *think and search* (text implicit)—the answer is in the text, but words used in the question and those in the answer are not in the same sentence; and *on my own* (experience-based)—the answer is not found in the text.

Teaching students to use QARs is based on four instructional principles: (1) give immediate feedback, (2) progress from shorter to longer texts, (3) begin with simple questions and progress to complex questions, and (4) develop independence by beginning with group learning exercises and progressing to individual, independent activities.

Raphael suggested teaching QARs in three stages. In stage one, consisting of four parts, QARs are introduced and practice is given at identifying task demands while answering questions. Short paragraphs are used with one question from each of the QAR categories accompanying them. Instruction proceeds from most support to least support. Students are given (1) the text, question, answer, QAR label, and reason why the label is appropriate; (2) the same information with instructions to generate their own reason for the appropriateness of the QAR label (immediate feedback is given to students on the accuracy and completeness of their reasoning); (3) the text, question, and answer with the request to supply the QAR label and their reasoning; and (4) the text and question with students expected to supply the rest of the missing information.

In stage two, students work through longer texts containing more questions. The teacher guides groups of students through an initial QAR as a review. Then, students work through the remaining exercises while the teacher provides feedback individually on QAR selection and answer accuracy.

In stage three, a chapter or full story is broken into four segments, each followed by six questions—two per QAR category. The first segment is a review done individually but corrected as a group. The remaining three segments are completed individually, with appropriate individual feedback. Because text selections do not necessarily support all types of questions, two questions per category are only a guide for teachers and students. Once students have successfully completed this stage, QARs can be maintained through consistent review and practice.

Using QARs allows students to independently analyze a text question and derive an appropriate answer. Once students gain independence in answering questions, teachers can teach them how to ask good questions. With QAR as a basis, we will describe a series of instructional strategies we believe will move students from dependence on the teacher to independence in asking their own questions as they read.

Directed Reading Activity

The Directed Reading Activity (DRA) is a teaching strategy developed as a comprehensive means of guiding students through a text selection and can be used as a unit-based or lesson-based strategy. As a unit-based strategy, the DRA can be tied more closely to the overarching central question that is asked of students as they deal with the text. Although there are a number of stages in the complete DRA strategy (see Tierney & Readence, 2000, for a discussion of the entire procedure), our central concern is the prereading, or readiness, stage of the lesson.

The prereading stage involves activating students' prior knowledge related to the text selection, creating motivation to read it, and setting the purpose(s) for reading. Questions can play an important role in preparing students to read the text.

Teachers can ask text implicit or experience-based questions to engage students' prior knowledge and stimulate their interest in the text. Even more crucial is asking a question or questions that will guide students through the entire text selection. If you do not give a specific reason for reading, students may treat all information as equally important and attempt to master it all. Teachers' overall concern in designing a purpose-setting question should be what students should know after they read the text. Once this is determined, focus students' attention on important information throughout the entire passage by asking appropriate questions. Thus, demonstration is one function of teacher questioning in the prereading stage of the DRA. Students cannot be expected to learn what effective questioning is without appropriate modeling.

The following sample text will be used to provide an example of the type of questions teachers might ask students before they read. This sample may not be typical of the length of text students may be assigned to read in their classes; bear in mind that it is being used for illustrative purposes.

Light From the Sun

The white light of the sun is made of red, orange, yellow, green, blue, and violet all mixed together. At noon when you look toward the sun, the sky looks white because you see all the colors at once. When you look upward away from the sun, the sky looks blue. The sunlight comes through a thin layer of air containing fine dust and water droplets. These small particles scatter the white light into its colors, but only the blue light comes down to earth.

At sunset, the sky often looks red. When the sun is low, its light must pass through more dust-filled air than when it is overhead. In the air close to the earth, dust particles are larger than they are in the upper air. These coarse particles scatter all colors except the reds. They give the sky a crimson glow.

Twenty miles above the earth, the air is very thin. Here the sky has no color at all. Even though the sun never sets in space, a day in space is blacker than our night. There is no daylight, for what we call that by name on earth is made up of thousands of reflections. However, even though space is black, we can see to read in it. A book, like the specks of dust or droplets of water in the earth's atmosphere, would reflect the light always streaming from the sun. (adapted from Branley, 1963)

Because teachers will decide what specific information deserves attention, let us assume that students will be expected to learn the following, listed in order of importance:

1. What we see on earth in daylight is caused by reflected light from the sun.

2. Even though outer space lacks daylight, we can see objects because of reflected light.

In asking questions about this text, teachers will attempt to activate students' prior knowledge about light from the sun and thus create interest in reading the text. Some students may lack sufficient knowledge to deal with these questions. However, the questions are intended to generate discussion and to find out what knowledge students possess. Because students have not yet read the text, the following questions might be asked.

1. What color is sunlight?
2. Why is the sky blue during the day and sometimes red at sunset?
3. Why can we see things during daylight?
4. What color is outer space?

These are representative of the kind of questions teachers should ask to activate prior knowledge and generate interest. Also, these questions enable teachers to introduce the material to be read and prime students for a purpose-setting question. Next, teachers might ask students the following questions to focus their attention on the major concepts when they do read the text:

5. Can you read a book if you are in a dark closet? Why or why not?
6. Can you read a book in the darkness of outer space?

By asking questions 5 and 6, teachers set up students for the purpose-setting question they need to answer as they read the text.

7. Why is it possible to read in outer space even though daylight does not exist there?

Such a question should increase students' anticipation of the text to be read and give teachers an opportunity to demonstrate the higher order question necessary to guide students through an assigned text.

Scaffolded Reading Experience

Another teaching strategy developed as a framework for guiding students through a text selection is the Scaffolded Reading Experience (SRE) (Graves & Graves, 1994). It, like the DRA, can be used as a means to enable teachers to ask appropriate questions of students before a text reading assignment. Also like the DRA, this strategy can function as a unit- or lesson-based strategy. Because the SRE is a comprehensive strategy designed as a set of prereading, reading, and postreading activities, interested readers should refer to Tierney and Readence (2000) for a complete discussion of the strategy. For the purposes of this book, we will be centrally concerned with the prereading activities suggested by Graves and Graves (1994).

The premise behind the SRE is the notion of scaffolding, or providing students with the necessary assistance in preparation, guidance, and follow-up to help them make connections with the text. According to Graves and Graves, what distinguishes the SRE from other instructional frameworks such as the DRA is that preset activities to use with text are not prescribed. Rather, SRE is viewed as a flexible framework that provides teachers with instructional options in which they are able to select the most appropriate activities to use with particular students, texts, and purposes for reading.

For instance, if sixth-grade students of average ability are to read a text on the development of the Declaration of Independence, and the purpose in reading the selection is to see how and why this document was written as it was, then in prereading a teacher might consider the use of a motivational activity, a vocabulary activity that introduces some new words, and a questioning activity that focuses students' attention on how particular groups of colonists influenced how the Declaration was written. This is to be contrasted with the lock-step activities of other strategies in which only preset activities take place in instruction. In the SRE prereading activities include, but might not be limited to

- activating background knowledge
- building text-specific knowledge
- direction setting
- motivating
- relating the reading to students' lives
- predicting
- prequestioning
- preteaching concepts
- preteaching vocabulary
- suggesting comprehension strategies

The selection of which activities to include is one done by the teacher through a consideration of the confines within which students are learning and the context in which that learning is to occur. Using too few activities might be inadequate to enhance students' learning, and using too many activities might be overkill. This flexibility in activity selection epitomizes the SRE. An examination of the activities mentioned as possibilities in prereading would indicate that asking and answering questions could be an important component of any lesson. Additionally, it should be mentioned that many of the activities to be described in future chapters of this book could be incorporated easily into the SRE. Chapter 7 will examine how to select and combine prereading activities into meaningful lessons.

Guided Practice in Student Questioning

Although teacher questions are of value in reading and learning from text, it is important for students to be able to generate their own questions in order to become independent learners. Promoting active comprehension through self-questioning helps students toward such independence.

The object of active comprehension is to provide students with practice in asking questions and to guide their thinking in learning from text before, during, and after reading. Singer and Donlan (1982) provided evidence that student-generated questions can lead to improved comprehension. They felt that generating questions entails a deeper processing of the text because students become more motivated and actively involved in the comprehension process.

The key to active comprehension is to guide instruction so skill in asking questions will transfer from teachers to students. Thus, a three-stage model is suggested for transfer of question asking: (1) modeling, (2) phase out/phase in strategies, and (3) active comprehension. Modeling is teachers showing students what constitutes good questioning behaviors. This involves taking students through lessons, demonstrating the kinds of questions to ask, and modeling the processes of thinking involved in designing questions. Phase out/phase in strategies (guided practice) occur when students are encouraged to progress through lessons that involve teacher guidance and provide a safe atmosphere in which students can ask questions in their efforts to comprehend the text. Gradually, teachers fade their guidance. As students begin to ask their own questions without teacher prompting, they are engaging in active comprehension (independent application). The advantage of having students actively generating their own questions about a text, as Ash (1992) has pointed out, is one way to ensure their engagement with, and interest in, text.

Using this three-stage model, we can see the teacher-originated questions in the DRA as a means by which to demonstrate effective question-asking behavior for students. Next, students are provided an environment that stimulates phase out/phase in strategies. Finally, strategies follow that focus on independent application and active comprehension. Our discussion of asking questions before reading follows this plan.

ReQuest

ReQuest, an abbreviation of *reciprocal questioning*, is a lesson-based strategy developed by Manzo (1969) to help students (1) formulate their own questions about the text they are reading, (2) develop an active inquiring attitude toward reading, (3) acquire purposes for their reading, and (4) develop independent comprehension abilities. ReQuest involves students and teacher silently reading portions of text and taking turns asking and answering questions concerning that material. It is the reciprocal nature of the questioning sequence that differentiates ReQuest from teacher-directed questioning strategies and provides the format for students' active involvement. Palincsar and Brown (1984) have shown that training in reciprocal questioning, in conjunction with use of other comprehension fostering activities, can promote students' comprehension of text.

The role of the teacher is central to the success of the ReQuest strategy. The teacher answers students' questions and serves as a model by asking thought-provoking questions that extend students' developing concepts. Thus, ReQuest can be conceived of as a phase out/phase in strategy in the model we are advocating. Teachers continue to demonstrate good questioning behaviors, and students gradually assume more responsibility in the questioning sequence as they become accustomed to the strategy. Thus, this strategy helps bridge the gap between teachers' modeling question-asking behavior for students and active comprehension through the use of students' own questions. The ReQuest technique consists of

- preparing the text
- readying the students
- developing questioning behaviors
- developing predictive behaviors
- reading silently
- discussing the reading

In preparing for ReQuest, be sure that the difficulty level of the text is suitable for the students and decide how much material will be read at one time (one sentence, one paragraph, etc.). The ability and maturity levels of the students dictate the amount of text to be read. Finally, identify appropriate points in the text where predictions will be elicited.

To provide an example of some aspects of ReQuest, a portion of our previously used sample passage, *Light From the Sun*, has been reproduced. For the sake of illustration, we will assume the passage is at the appropriate difficulty level and that it has been decided to be read only one sentence at a time. Two points, designated (P1) and (P2), have been identified where the teacher can elicit predictions from the students about the passage.

Light From the Sun

The white light of the sun is made of red, orange, yellow, green, blue, and violet all mixed together. At noon when you look toward the sun, the sky looks white because you see all the colors at once. (P1) When you look upward away from the sun, the sky looks blue. The sunlight comes through a thin layer of air containing fine dust and water droplets. (P2) These small particles scatter the white light into its colors, but only the blue light comes down to earth.

Prepare the students by giving them the guidelines for ReQuest. It also may be necessary to acquaint students with any new vocabulary in the text and to create interest or develop background for the reading. Having students read the title and tell you what they know about the topic would suffice in many cases.

Following silent reading, students ask questions of the teacher. The teacher answers the questions and, in turn, refines and extends the developing concepts by asking questions of students. For instance, after reading sentence one of our sample text, ask, "What colors are in white?" In this way students are able to generalize the notion that white is made up of many colors.

Similarly, after reading sentence two, ask students, "If white light comes from the sun, why do you think the sky around it is only blue?" To reemphasize, the reciprocal nature of questioning in this technique is what differentiates ReQuest from more traditional questioning strategies.

When a sufficient amount of the text has been read, predictions about the outcome of the selection are elicited from the students. Students also must provide justifications for their predictions. In the case of our sample text, it was decided to ask for predictions early (P1) because the topic is straightforward and the leading question would lead to predicting the content. The second prediction point (P2) was chosen as a backup in the event students were unable to generate predictions at P1.

Once predictions are generated, justified, and discussed, students silently read the rest of the text to verify their predictions. After the reading, discuss the text with the prime focus being the reconsideration of the students' predictions about the outcome of the selection.

By formulating their own questions about a text and trying to construct questions to extend the teacher's thinking, students become actively involved in the comprehension process before they read the material. Eliciting student predictions serves as the culmination of this prereading strategy as it leads students to tie together what they know in order to formulate those predictions. Students then read with greater readiness as they attempt to verify their predictions.

When ReQuest is first used, students ask many text explicit questions. It is here that teachers ask questions on higher levels of comprehension to act as a model and to help students integrate the text material they are reading with their prior knowledge of the topic. Thus, you can be assured that students will be introduced to the major concepts to be learned from the text. Simultaneously, teachers are beginning the phase out/phase in strategy of active comprehension. Through the reciprocal nature of ReQuest, students gradually learn to ask thought-provoking questions as question-asking responsibility shifts to them through repeated experiences with the strategy. This transfer may be further promoted by QAR training, having students work in pairs or small groups without teacher guidance, and asking questions of one another using the procedural steps of ReQuest. This premise has been suggested by Helfeldt and Henk (1990) through the use of a strategy called ReQAR (Reciprocal Question-Answer Relationships).

Perhaps a greater impetus to students' independent question-asking ability would be to have them take a more dominant role in asking questions about a text and in setting a purpose. The next strategy described, the Directed Reading-Thinking Activity, attempts to provide students such an opportunity.

Directed Reading-Thinking Activity

The Directed Reading-Thinking Activity (DRTA) (Stauffer, 1969) enables students to take a more dominant role in preparing themselves to read a text as teachers become moderators. Used as either a lesson-based or unit-based strategy, the DRTA is based on the notion that students will develop their abilities to predict, connect, and organize text information while they read and will continually refine their purposes as they use their prior knowledge to understand text. The DRTA begins with the generation of hypotheses for reading and continues with the refinement of these hypotheses as new information is extracted from text. In essence, the reader poses questions, tests these questions while reading the text, generates new questions, and modifies previous predictions as reading progresses.

The DRTA consists of (1) directing the reading-thinking process and (2) fundamental skill training. The first element entails setting purposes for reading, reading to verify those purposes, pausing to evaluate understanding, and then proceeding to read with the new purposes. The second element consists of students reexamining the text to learn to effectively use reading skills such as word recognition, contextual analysis, and concept development. The focus of the discussion is on the initial phase of the DRTA—directing students' reading-thinking behaviors to promote active comprehension.

Essentially, directing the reading-thinking behaviors of students involves three steps: (1) predicting, (2) reading, and (3) proving. Teachers should divide the text to be read into appropriate segments. Students proceed through a segment of text to define purposes for reading and to evaluate and revise these purposes using the information they acquire. Teachers act as facilitators of this process.

Using the *Light From the Sun* example, students can be directed to read the title, examine any accompanying pictures or diagrams, and make predictions as to the content of the text selection. Encourage them to offer different suggestions and to critically evaluate these suggestions. Then direct students to read a segment of text to check their predictions. It should be noted that vocabulary is not introduced prior to reading; therefore, students should be encouraged to use the context to figure out any unknown words they may encounter.

After they have read the initial segment, direct students to close their texts. Then begin an examination of the evidence. Previous predictions about the content should be evaluated in light of new information. Ask students to provide proof of their predictions, and read text segments orally for verification. If evidence causes students to refine their predictions, new predictions should be generated. Students then should be directed to read a new segment of text, and the predicting, reading, and proving cycles continue. As reading progresses, predictions, which at first may be divergent, generally will converge as more information is amassed. Once predictions about the text converge, direct students to read the rest of the selection on their own.

The DRTA is adaptable to the given text situation, as Bear and McIntosh (1990) have demonstrated. They describe four types of DRTAs: (1) Table of Contents DRTA, (2) Whole Book DRTA, (3) Chapter DRTA, and (4) No Book DRTA. The DRTA can be modified depending on the purpose of the lesson, the length of the material, or whether the teacher wants to get an assessment of students' prior knowledge of a topic before any reading occurs.

The DRTA goes beyond the reciprocal give and take of ReQuest. Teachers fade their demonstration of effective questioning behavior and provide guided practice for students as they formulate their own purpose-setting questions about the text.

Survey Technique

The final strategy of this chapter, the Survey Technique (Aukerman, 1972), is a unit-based, whole-class adaptation of the initial step of the SQ3R study method. Students do a text preview and systematically analyze the various graphic aids present in a reading assignment and use their prior knowledge to formulate purposes for reading. The purposes generated should be tied directly to the central question of the unit posed to the students by the teacher. This prereading strategy consists of

- analyzing the chapter title
- analyzing the chapter headings
- analyzing the visual aids
- reading the introductory paragraph
- reading the concluding paragraph
- deriving the main idea

Before students begin to read the text assignment, ask them to analyze the chapter title to discuss what might be included. Next, students should skim through the chapter to locate and read any chapter headings. The class should devise a question to be answered by reading that subsection. Students interpret graphs, maps, and charts for the gist of the information they summarize. Pictures are discussed to determine what they represent.

Next, ask students to silently read the introductory and concluding paragraphs of the chapter. These paragraphs usually provide readers with some general ideas about the content of the chapter. A brief discussion following their reading is recommended. In addition, students might examine the postreading questions provided at the chapter's end. Students should have a good idea of the chapter's contents by this time, so end the Survey Technique by having the students list ideas to be discussed in the chapter. From this, students develop a main statement about the overall theme of the chapter. At this point, students are prepared to enter the text more thoroughly.

This prereading strategy should take about 30 minutes of classroom instructional time. During this time, demonstrate the strategy by explaining how to analyze the various parts of the text. We recommend that a time limit be imposed once students are familiar with the procedure. This necessitates skimming for information. Students then can independently survey the text chapter for information. A whole-group discussion would follow to pool students' ideas, culminating with a purpose-setting question. In this way students get feedback on the ideas others are getting from the text and see how these ideas are organized into a main idea statement. Once students are able to verbalize what they are doing, they should not need teacher guidance, thus achieving the goal of active comprehension.

Summary

This chapter provides a rationale for the use of questions in a prereading situation to stimulate curiosity, to aid students in activating prior knowledge and anticipating information, and to focus attention on important information. Unit-based and lesson-based strategies have been recommended, which will allow you to provide guidance in the use of questioning and then to gradually withdraw your guidance until the expected learning outcome of using questions to set purposes for reading is achieved by your students. Active comprehension results, and students can use self-questioning to independently learn from text.

Chapter 3

Forecasting Passages

PURPOSE

This chapter demonstrates the use of prediction as a means of motivating students, activating prior knowledge, and highlighting important concepts.

Strategies

1. The *Anticipation Guide* is designed to enhance comprehension by encouraging students to elaborate concepts in text about which they may have prior knowledge.

2. *Story Impressions* have students predict and write a story line when given a list of key concepts from a text.

3. *Text Previews* allow students a quick method for surveying a text chapter before reading in order to develop links to information previously learned and to make decisions about how they will read the chapter.

4. *Analogies* enhance student learning by comparing a new concept to one that is already familiar.

5. The *PreReading Plan* provides students the opportunity to brainstorm about ideas to be presented in the text; to develop associations related to these ideas; and to elaborate, reflect, and rethink these ideas.

6. The *Visual Reading Guide* introduces students to a passage by examining the charts, graphs, diagrams, maps, and illustrations to formulate predictions about information in a text.

Readers must rely on forecasting (predicting) to make sense of the passage to be read. Prediction is an essential process in several models of reading (see Ruddell, Ruddell, & Singer, 1994). Before reading, students must have some idea of what to expect in order to compare their expectations to what is being processed during reading. If the information being read is expected, the reading process is fluid, with optimal comprehension. If the information read is not expected, some decisions must be made.

Before reading a chapter on the solar system, students formulate some hypotheses about what they expect to be reading. They may expect the text to give a general description of the solar system, discuss the sun, and then present information about individual planets, including temperature characteristics, makeup of the atmosphere, and number and size of satellites. As long as this is generally what students see, there is no problem. They probably will read some information they already know, plus some new information they may or may not find interesting and important.

But what happens if students read a sentence that states that the Earth's moon is made of green cheese? Based on the predictions the students have made, this information was not expected in a scientific discussion of the planets. Students have several options. One is to form an alternative plan to accept the information as fact and change their understanding of the moon; another is to trust initial impressions and try to combine prior knowledge with new information in a way that makes sense. Finally, students can assume that either they misread the passage or the author made an error. By rereading the statement, students finally see that the statement was read out of context and the author was stating that, in the past, people had believed the moon to be made of green cheese.

Forecasting a passage necessitates some uncertainty. Students cannot be sure that the information presented in a passage either will meet their expectations or will be wrong. Students also may discover that, although the author's information is correct, it is not presented in the expected format. Then, students must have enough flexibility to modify their expectations in order to understand the information presented in the passage.

Students who had not formed predictions about the information to be read probably would not have noticed any inconsistency in the passage. Unfortunately, many students read this way. They may have the prior knowledge necessary to understand the passage but the information is useless unless it is activated before reading. Students who do not forecast a passage have no expectations. When inconsistent information is presented, reading continues. No internal flag is raised to inform them that something is not making sense. Students then have trouble figuring out why the teacher will not accept their explanation of the topic being discussed.

Finally, students can take the safe route and not read. Unfortunately, many students take this path. Forecasting demands risk taking and some students are afraid to risk being wrong. Although this attitude is safe, it defeats the purposes of education.

Fortunately, there are many strategies available to teachers to foster these predicting skills. Some of these strategies are quite simple. For instance, a teacher could read the beginning of a story or a passage aloud to students, stopping just before an important idea has been presented. The students could guess what they think is going to happen, then the teacher could assign students to complete the reading in order to see if their predictions were realized. Teachers who use problem-based learning also can foster this skill by posing central questions to students prior to learning in order to arouse students' curiosity to seek answers. For example, a teacher could ask students, "Is it ever possible to achieve world peace?" prior to a lesson on world conflict. Inviting guest speakers into a classroom also can pique students' interest in learning, as they set individual purposes for reading based on information and ideas from the presentation (Brozo & Simpson, 1999). Additional strategies for involving students in forecasting passages are presented in this chapter.

Anticipation Guide

The Anticipation Guide is designed to enhance comprehension by encouraging students to focus attention on concepts to be covered in the text. Challenging students' prior knowledge arouses curiosity. Lunstrum (1981) discussed the use of controversy in motivating students to read in the content areas. Misconceptions students might have related to the content become the center for discussion and debate, forcing students to justify, modify, or delete prior knowledge. Prior knowledge then becomes the focus for predictions that will guide students through the passage.

The Anticipation Guide is a lesson-based or unit-based strategy that can be used with students at all levels with a variety of print and non-print media. The chosen topic should be one about which students already have prior knowledge; totally unfamiliar topics are difficult to discuss. An Anticipation Guide is designed to prepare students to focus on specific concepts by creating a mismatch between their prior knowledge and the information to be learned. The overall purpose for reading becomes an attempt to resolve these differences.

The following steps can be used in the construction and implementation of an Anticipation Guide (Head & Readence, 1992). Each step is illustrated with an example pertaining to ecology.

1. *Identify the major concepts to be learned.* Analyze the content of the passage to decide the major points to be emphasized. You do not want students to memorize every fact in a text; the goal is for students to be able to identify and understand the major ideas. In a passage on the environment, the text focuses on different types of pollution and on the potential limitations of natural resources. The following concepts were identified as the most important for students to understand after the unit was completed.

   - There are limitations to the quantity and quality of our natural resources.
   - Alternate forms of energy need to be developed.
   - Our lives are being violated by many types of pollution involving land, water, air, and noise.
   - People are responsible for their environment.

2. *Determine whether the main concepts will support or challenge students' beliefs.* You must decide what kinds of experiential backgrounds students possess related to the topic. (This process is discussed in Chapter 1.) Parents' attitudes, community values, and socioeconomic factors should be considered. Students whose parents are employed by a nuclear power plant might feel quite different about nuclear energy from students whose parents are antinuclear activists. It is important to respect individual students and not try to influence them to align with your opinions. Students generally are reticent about volunteering opinions once teachers have expressed their feelings.

3. *Create three to five statements to support or challenge students' opinions.* The number of statements will vary depending on the age of the students, level of topic familiarity, and number of major concepts. However, because each statement will be closely examined and discussed, three to five statements are plenty.

Step 3 is one of the most crucial and is more difficult than it may seem initially. Good statements are most effective when opinion rather than fact influence students' prior knowledge about the topic. When students are familiar with the topic, discussion is less effective. A common error in constructing Anticipation Guide statements is to use a factual sentence. A statement such as "The Environmental Protection Agency is housed in the Department of Agriculture" is dry, boring, and difficult to discuss. Students either know that it is correct or incorrect, or they have no idea of the answer.

The following Anticipation Guide was constructed based on the major concepts identified in Step 1.

Directions: Before reading the following passage about ecology and the environment, read each of the following statements carefully. Put a check next to each one with which you agree. Be ready to discuss your decisions.

_____ a. There is little we can do to save our environment.

_____ b. Advancing technology is more important than protecting the environment.

_____ c. Nuclear power is the answer to our energy needs.

_____ d. Air pollution affects us all.

4. *Arrange the statements in the order you find to be the most appropriate and decide on a presentation method.* The order of the statements could parallel their presentation in the text, or they could be arranged to allow for optimal discussion, that is, most important to least important. The Anticipation Guide can be presented effectively through the use of overhead transparencies, chalkboards, or photocopies. Include spaces for students to mark responses and give directions appropriate for the level of the students.

5. *Present the Guide to the students.* Directions and statements should be read to the students before they work independently. Stress that students must be ready to defend their opinions during follow-up discussions.

There are alternate methods for presenting the Anticipation Guide. One method is to have two columns before each statement, the first labeled *Me* and the second labeled *Author.* Students fill in the first column. While reading the text, students try to take on the role of the author, filling in the statements as they believe the author would. This format is illustrated here.

Me Author

___ ___ There is little we can do to save our environment.

___ ___ Advancing technology is more important than protecting the environment.

___ ___ Nuclear power is the answer to our energy needs.

___ ___ Air pollution affects us all.

Another method is to label the first column *Anticipation* and the second column *Reaction*. Before reading, students write their responses in the Anticipation column. After reading, students respond in the Reaction column. A combination of these two modifications is possible using three columns labeled *Anticipation, Author,* and *Reaction.* Students respond before reading, read critically to determine the author's point of view, and then react after reading.

6. *Discuss each statement.* Discussion can take many forms. A good way to begin is to ask students to raise their hands if they agree or disagree with the statement. Volunteers from each group try to convince members of the opposing group to switch sides. Even quiet students can compare their thoughts with those of others in both groups and can mentally evaluate their own statements. Discussion continues until each viewpoint has been considered and evaluated by the class. Another vote can be taken to see if anyone changed opinions.

A method more suitable for more mature students is to form discussion groups of four to six students. The members of the group must reach a consensus on each statement. If they cannot, they must explain why. After the groups have finished, a whole-class discussion follows. This discussion can focus on getting the class to reach a consensus based on discussion from within the groups. It is important to note that agreement is not necessary, but students must try to analyze why they cannot reach agreement.

7. *Direct students to read the text.* The purpose for reading the text is now built in. Students will read to find out if the information to be learned agrees with their thoughts and also to find additional information that will allow them to support, deny, or modify their original thoughts.

8. *Follow-up discussion.* After reading, the class may get together to respond to the same statements using additional information gleaned from the text. If the me/author format is used, the discussion can focus on similarities and differences between student and author responses, answering questions such as, On which statements did you agree? Disagree? Why do you think the author does not agree with you? Did you change your mind as you read the passage? Do you still disagree with the author? Why? What could the author have done to convince you to

change your opinion? What could you tell the author to try to change his/her opinion? If the anticipation/reaction format is used, similarities and differences between the two columns can be explored and discussed. The students should explain exactly what made them change their minds and should be ready to defend their new opinions.

The Anticipation Guide can be diagnostic in scope, assessing the prior knowledge of individual students. During the class discussion, individuals may be identified who would profit from alternative pre-reading or enrichment activities that expand on the subject to ensure an awareness of major concepts. Possible groupings of individuals may become apparent before valuable instructional time is used. Students who already display a firm grasp of the textual knowledge may be shifted to alternative areas of study.

Because the Anticipation Guide is teacher directed and is based on information about which students have little prior knowledge, this strategy does not always lend itself to fading as well as some of the other strategies mentioned. However, the notion of having students ask themselves questions about the topic before they read (as discussed in Chapter 2) can be practiced through the use of the Anticipation Guide. After demonstrating the Guide's construct, you could ask students with prior knowledge of the topic to help in the construction of the Guide, thus leading students to independent construction. Through group consensus, the best statements could be prepared for the rest of the class. In this way, some students could use their expertise to help others lacking mastery of the topic. Students also might lend a unique interpretation to the topic—one you had not considered previously.

Story Impressions

Another teaching strategy that involves using anticipation in order to arouse students' curiosity is Story Impressions (McGinley & Denner, 1987). In this lesson-based strategy, the teacher lists clue words or important phrases from a passage or story, and students write their impression of how they think the words will fit together prior to reading. By trying to piece together story elements prior to reading, students are forming a prediction of how characters and events unfold. The goal is not to correctly guess how a story will unfold, but to compare how each student guesses a story is organized and compare it to the author's version.

There are six steps in completing a Story Impressions lesson:

1. *Introduce students to the Story Impressions strategy.* Tell them that, "Today we are going to talk about what we think the story we are going to read could be about before we read it."

2. *Show students the clue words on a transparency or on the chalkboard.* For example, using the book *Faithful Elephants* (Tsuchiya, 1951/1988), students would look at the following:

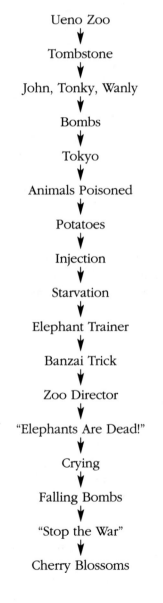

Ueno Zoo
↓
Tombstone
↓
John, Tonky, Wanly
↓
Bombs
↓
Tokyo
↓
Animals Poisoned
↓
Potatoes
↓
Injection
↓
Starvation
↓
Elephant Trainer
↓
Banzai Trick
↓
Zoo Director
↓
"Elephants Are Dead!"
↓
Crying
↓
Falling Bombs
↓
"Stop the War"
↓
Cherry Blossoms

3. *Students read the clues together and try to brainstorm how the arrows link together the story elements.* The goal here is to try to predict or forecast how all the story elements might come together.

4. *The class dictates a story by using the ideas generated in Step 3.* The teacher acts as a facilitator in writing ideas dictated by the class. Using the *Faithful Elephants* example, a dictated story could look like the following:

> At the Ueno Zoo in Tokyo, three men named John, Tonky, and Wanly set off a bomb under a tombstone. Many animals were hurt and some were killed. The bomb contained poisoned potatoes, and some of the animals were poisoned. They were given an injection to counteract the poison, but some did not recover and could not eat anything. The elephant trainer did not want them to die of starvation, so he tried a banzai trick to get them to eat, but it didn't work with the elephants. The zoo director shouted, "The elephants are dead," and all the children at the zoo were crying. John, Tonky, and Wanly were not happy with the destruction, so they made more bombs and dropped them off a bridge near the zoo. The falling bombs went off right under the cherry trees, and cherry blossoms blew up everywhere. The zoo director issued a plea in the newspaper for the three men to "Stop the War."

5. *The class compares and contrasts the Story Impression with the actual story.* Students then read the story individually or orally with the idea of examining their story with the original. You could use a compare/contrast Graphic Organizer as part of the process (discussed in Chapter 5) to record students' ideas.

6. *Once students are familiar with the Story Impressions strategy, they could write individual story predictions or work in small groups.*

Story Impressions also can be used effectively with informational text, with the teacher recording key terms and phrases from a textbook chapter and having students write predictions about how they think the elements will be integrated.

Text Previews

The Text Preview (Graves, Cooke, & LaBerge, 1983) is a lesson-based or unit-based strategy that is similar to the Anticipation Guide and Story Impressions, in that the goals are to motivate students to read and to provide an organizational framework from which students can comprehend a text. In addition, this strategy attempts to enhance students' background knowledge related to the topic of study by expanding what students know prior to reading. Tierney and Readence (2000) suggest that there are two major stages to be used in implementing Text Previews in the classroom.

1. *Preparing and constructing the Text Preview.* The Text Preview should contain three elements. First, there should be an interest-building section, in which several rhetorical questions are asked to pique students' interest in the text that is going to be read. Second, a brief synopsis of the text is provided, in which students may be introduced to the main characters, setting, and a short discussion related to the theme of the passage. Third, students are provided with purpose-setting questions or directions that they can use while reading the passage. For example, suppose students are going to be reading the book *Good Night, Mr. Tom* (Magorian, 1981). The following Text Preview could serve as an introduction to the book:

   > Being away from home to live in an unfamiliar place can be scary, especially when you are not with anyone you know. You are among people who act differently and have different customs from what you are used to, and you might be afraid that you will make a mistake in front of those you are trying to impress. You might also feel unwelcome, and wish that you could return to the comfort and friends in your hometown. Have you even moved to a new location? Do you know what it feels like to be the "new kid" who everyone seems to be watching? How did the situation make you feel?
   >
   > In the book we will begin to read in class, you will be introduced to an 8-year-old boy named Willie Beech, who has been evacuated from London just before World War II is about to break out. His abusive mother has sent him to live in the country, where she feels he will be safe. Government authorities place him with a man named Mr. Tom Oakley. Willie has never been out of the city, and as he enters Mr. Tom's cottage, he is shivering from cold and fear.
   >
   > What would living in this new environment be like? Would Mr. Tom beat Willie as his mother had done? How will Willie possibly survive all alone? You will have to read the story to find out.

2. *Presentation of the Text Preview.* Once the Text Preview is made up, it is presented to the students. This stage is simple and straightforward. Tell students they are going to be reading a new story, then read the interest-building section of the Text Preview and initiate a class discussion in which students relate similar

experiences and respond to the questions. Then read the remainder of the Text Preview and encourage students to begin reading the selection.

Text Previews also can be used with informational text. The interest-building section can be related to historical events or scientific or mathematical concepts. After a brief synopsis allowing students to acquire some background information, you can give them purpose-setting questions to guide their subsequent reading. Older students also can use teacher-made Text Previews independently. You can ask them to think about interest-building statements and questions, and you can leave space on a handout for students to respond before they read the remainder of the preview. Chen and Graves (1998) discussed additional ways this strategy can be used with ESL students.

Analogies

Teaching with analogies allows teachers to make connections between new ideas and students' background knowledge (Glynn, 1996). Quite simply, analogies provide a means for thinking about the unknown by using something that is more well known. For example, a student might not be familiar with the sport of cricket, but he or she may know a good deal about baseball. By using a baseball analogy to learn about cricket, learners can remember more than if they did not link the two sports (Hayes & Tierney, 1982). Analogies have proven to be effective learning tools for reinforcing thinking skills and conceptual understanding (Alvermann & Phelps, 1998).

In constructing analogies, try to use real-life incidents to which students can relate. Thus, the students will have the basis for forming a comparison to the new information that is going to be studied. Questions related to the analogy can help engage students in thinking about the text and arouse their curiosity, similar to the previous strategies described in this chapter.

Analogies can be created for almost any lesson or unit in any content area. Unit-based analogies can focus students' attention on central questions. For example, students who are going to be studying the Civil War in a social studies class might be introduced to the following analogy concerning the family:

Have you ever had a fight with someone in your family? Have you ever been so angry with your brothers or sisters that you yelled at them or hit them? Have you ever been so angry at something they did that you were mad at them for a long time? Did you wonder if you would ever get along with them again? When the United States entered into the Civil War, it was a similar situation. Confederate supporters in the southern states were angry with Union supporters from the northern states. The South wanted to break away from the United States and form their own country. Many people were caught in the middle. Robert E. Lee was a good example. He had been an important leader in the United States Army, and had been asked by President Lincoln to head the Union Army. The problem was that General Lee was from Virginia, a state that had joined the Confederacy. How could he choose sides against his friends and family from home? How could he turn against his President and his country?

Encourage students to formulate their own analogies in their thinking and writing as they move through the cycle of instruction. Analogies can prove to be powerful tools for learning and remembering, especially for unfamiliar concepts.

PreReading Plan

The PreReading Plan (PReP) was developed by Langer (1981) as a lesson-based method of using and analyzing students' prior knowledge. Teachers can use the information gained from the prereading lesson to tailor instruction to meet the needs of students at all grade levels. PReP can be used to prepare students to read, to view a movie or film, observe a classroom demonstration, or prepare for a field trip.

There are two major phases to implementing PReP in the classroom (Tierney & Readence, 2000). The first phase involves engaging students in a discussion of the key concepts relating to the topic. Teachers must decide on which concepts to emphasize and on ways to elicit student discussion based on those concepts. (Chapter 1 details how teachers may develop expected learning outcomes.) The discussion occurs in three steps.

1. *Initial associations with the concept.* In this step teachers encourage students to elaborate about their prior knowledge on the topic. For instance, in presenting a lesson on space exploration you might ask, "What kinds of things come to mind when you think about the exploration of outer space? What would it be like to be an astronaut landing on an uncharted planet? What would you expect to see? Hear? Feel? Smell? Would you be afraid or anxious?" As students generate responses, write them on the chalkboard.

These questions should be divergent enough to allow students to recall a variety of prior information related to the topic.

2. *Reflecting on initial associations.* During this part of the discussion, students reflect and elaborate on the ideas generated in Step 1. They should explain their responses. You may ask, "Why would it be scary to be on an uncharted planet? Why do you think it would be quiet? Why do you think the planet would have no inhabitants? What things would make you afraid?" During this part of the discussion students clarify their ideas related to the topic. Students should be aware that there may not be agreement among all class members, but that is not a problem because each person will have his or her own associations.

3. *Reformulate knowledge.* During this phase of the discussion, the teacher asks students if they have new insights into the topic based on discussion in Steps 1 and 2, or if they wish to change any of the ideas previously presented. After the discussion in Step 3, students often come up with new associations not considered initially. Students are allowed to add, delete, or modify ideas.

In the second phase of PReP, the teacher analyzes the responses of individual students to assess the extent of individual knowledge related to the topic to be studied. Any misinformation a student may have that might cause problems with a lesson is noted. For instance, a student's comment about going to Jupiter for a weekend vacation may indicate that she does not understand the length of time needed to travel through space, or her comment may be creative speculation.

During this analysis phase, the teacher can plan the best ways to teach the material to students. If many students have prior knowledge related to the topic to be studied, you may want to include additional enrichment activities, or perhaps abbreviate sections of the chapter. The opposite may also happen. If you feel that most of the students are not ready to begin this unit, some background teaching may be necessary to ensure optimal learning.

Although PReP (like the Anticipation Guide) is mainly teacher-directed, the concepts behind PReP can be more easily transferred to student control. Through brainstorming prior knowledge, reflecting on the ideas, and reformulating thoughts, students can use the three discussion steps to question themselves before reading information from text. The teacher could informally critique students at each step, challenging them to preview lessons by relating prior knowledge to the topic of study. Students could be encouraged to independently apply PReP to difficult lessons in content areas. You should emphasize the value of taking time for this prereading activity. A common complaint among students is, "You mean I still have to read it after all that?" If through teacher modeling, demonstration, and guided practice students can see the value in such an exercise, they are more likely to use this strategy.

Visual Reading Guide

The Visual Reading Guide (VRG) (Stein, 1978) is an approach for introducing students to a passage by predicting information based on graphics contained in the text. As designed, the VRG is a lesson-based instructional activity that helps students draw connections between information presented in graphic aids, the text, and prior knowledge. Many times students ignore charts, maps, diagrams, and photographs, even though these text elements offer important information that leads to understanding. Students seem to think that because these visuals are not covered on a test and are seldom discussed in class, they can be skipped. Students welcome photographs because they take up space and make chapters shorter.

Using the VRG, the teacher assesses expected learning outcomes, deciding which visuals support the information presented in the text and which maps or charts present information relating to the major concepts to be presented. Some graphics are not used in the VRG because they do not relate information essential to understanding the text. They may be helpful, but they are not really necessary to understanding main ideas presented in text. Students are bombarded with information while reading, so the teacher's job is to realistically limit the amount of information for which students will be held accountable. Presenting the VRG to students involves the following steps:

1. *Identification.* Explain to students why some graphics are more important than others. What are the qualities that make one chart important and another optional? When students are reading independently, this skill is crucial.

2. *Analysis.* Students should ascertain what each graphic is depicting. Some may have titles or headings, but these are not always accurate. Students should try to answer questions such as, What is this showing me? How is this graphic organized? Why is this

important to the topic we will be studying? Is there anything here that does not make sense? Why?

3. *Discussion.* After the graphic has been analyzed for content, students should try to use the information to formulate a main idea, citing supporting evidence for their statement. As in the Anticipation Guide, students should try to reach a group consensus concerning information portrayed in the visual. To increase student involvement, display the visual without its heading and ask students to supply information based on their prior knowledge.

Each visual is identified, analyzed, and discussed using the steps outlined. With teacher aid, students should be able to learn what to expect in a passage and to learn its important concepts. They will understand your expected learning outcomes and the content knowledge needed to understand the graphic.

Unlike the other strategies mentioned in this chapter, the VRG lends itself to the cycle instruction and fading. You could model the strategy by explaining why some graphics are more important than others. This gives students an insight into the types of information you find important in the text. Through class discussions and guided practice, students gain insights into how the teacher and other students analyze visuals. This is particularly useful for those who may have problems understanding charts, maps, and diagrams. As slower students listen to the explanations of others, they gain their own insights into the information and they learn the thinking processes of more able students.

You can aid the transfer of responsibility to students by gradually turning over more of the class discussion to them. At first, you may want to identify the important graphics, explain why each is important, discuss what the visuals show, and explain their importance to the topic (modeling). After students become familiar with this routine, limit your participation by identifying only the important graphics and allow the students to analyze and discuss each (guided practice). The end result is to have students independently identify, analyze, and explain the graphics important in understanding the topic being studied. This skill is especially useful for high school and college students who are responsible for large amounts of reading. The VRG may allow these students to focus on information related to the main ideas in the text. The goal is to create readers who can function independently of the teacher in the world outside of school.

Summary

This chapter presents a rationale for the importance of activating prior knowledge before reading in order to predict meaning. Forecasting information in a passage allows the reader to form expectations that will guide the reading to follow. If the information being presented is consistent with expectations, the reading process is fluid; if the information is not consistent, the good reader learns to take steps to correct the inconsistencies. In addition, making predictions can pique students' interests and arouse their curiosity, which in turn provides them with the motivation to learn new information. Six strategies that allow students to activate prior knowledge in order to forecast a passage have been presented. These strategies conform to the five factors presented in Chapter 1 that affect learning from text: expected learning outcomes, motivation, content knowledge, attention, and learning strategies. Suggestions were outlined for transferring these skills to promote independent learning.

Chapter 4

Understanding Vocabulary

PURPOSE

This chapter demonstrates the necessity of understanding new vocabulary in text to enhance students' comprehension and describes teaching and learning strategies that capitalize on context and categorization as ways to determine the meanings of new vocabulary.

Strategies

1. *Contextual Redefinition* helps students use context to make informed guesses about word meanings.
2. *Possible Sentences* aids students in predicting the meanings of unknown words and verifying their accuracy.
3. *List-Group-Label* activates students' prior knowledge about related concepts to be encountered in text.
4. *Feature Analysis* uses categorization as a systematic means of introducing and reinforcing word meanings.

Vocabulary knowledge plays a central role in reading comprehension. Not only does common sense tell us this, but research points out that students' knowledge of words predicts their comprehension of passages (Ruddell, 1994). Although there are many distinct views on why vocabulary knowledge is a major factor in passage comprehension, we do know that the number of word meanings readers know directly relates to their ability to comprehend text.

A search of the professional literature provides various recommendations for increasing students' vocabulary. Many strategies are available to acquaint students with new vocabulary such as vocabulary notebooks, increased free-reading time, and discussing new terms as they are encountered. In many cases, these strategies entail developing content knowledge prior to reading. The strategies also provide the structure for teachers to fade their guidance so students can use them independently.

Why Introduce New Vocabulary?

Readence, Bean, and Baldwin (1998) state that the role of content teachers should be to help students become *insiders* in their interaction with textbooks and subject matter. The following paragraph illustrates this point:

> Sometimes a mob might "grift" all day without "turning them over" but this is unlikely except in the case of a "jug mob" which takes a limited number of "pokes." Any pickpocket who has on his person more than one wallet is something of a hazard both to himself and to the mob, for each wallet can count as a separate offense if he should be caught. Therefore, it is safer to have cash only. "Class mobs" usually count the money each time they "skin the pokes," one stall commonly is responsible for all of it, and an accounting in full is made at the end of the day. When there is a woman with the mob, she usually carries the "knock up." (Maurer, 1955, p. 194)

Were you able to deal effectively with the terminology of the passage, or did you feel like an outsider due to your lack of awareness about pickpockets? Outsiders are restricted in their communication with a group because they cannot use the group's special vocabulary and the concepts inherent in that terminology. Insiders use special vocabulary freely to communicate with the collective members of a group. The analogy here is that students may be outsiders in the fields of science, social studies, or mathematics. They need to become insiders with the concepts of these subjects, and, to a large extent, this can be accomplished by introducing students to the technical vocabulary of these subjects.

Another argument for introducing the vocabulary of a content area is that *knowing* a word is not an all or nothing proposition. Using the term *gold* as an example, most people probably would feel confident of its meaning and would know how to use the word in ordinary conversation. However, as in the pickpocket example, one would not feel so confident about knowing the meaning of gold when in the company of an ingroup such as jewelers or metallurgists. Additionally, you probably think of gold as a yellowish colored precious metal, but this is not necessarily true. First, not all gold is a yellowish color; second, if a mountain of gold were discovered, it no longer would be considered precious. Thus, a word is defined by its context.

This notion ties directly into how a word will be defined in this chapter. A *word* is a pattern of auditory or visual symbols that represent schemata (Readence, Bean, & Baldwin, 1998). Such a definition implies that word meanings are in an endless stage of flux as the concepts words represent are being modified constantly by our daily life and classroom experiences. Content teachers should introduce the essential vocabulary students need to activate the appropriate schemata and enhance their comprehension of text.

Acquiring New Vocabulary

Vocabulary knowledge may be acquired through direct or indirect experiences. Direct experience occurs when students personally interact with what they are to learn. For instance, science students may learn the concept of *refraction* by conducting an experiment with light and glass. This is the best way of learning new words, beginning at an early age. Vocabulary also may be acquired through indirect experiences, including watching films and television programs, looking at pictures, and experiencing other media.

However, there are some concepts that cannot be learned either by direct or indirect experience. These are words that must be learned by making connections to known words. For instance, the concepts of *communism* or *depression* must be learned symbolically through association with other known vocabulary concepts. Not surprisingly, many of the words to be learned in content texts have to be learned symbolically. The prereading activities described in this chapter will help students learn new vocabulary symbolically by associating them with known vocabulary in context or through categorization.

Principles of Vocabulary Instruction

First, students do not automatically acquire new concepts and the ability to identify words that represent new concepts on their own. Direct instruction is essential, and almost any kind of instruction is better than none at all. In fact, the provision of the meanings of words, practicing their meanings, and learning meanings from context will be better than no instruction for most adolescent readers. Therefore, a second principle of effective vocabulary instruction is to provide students with instruction for potentially troublesome words.

Third, the importance of practice with new words cannot be underestimated. Students should be given an opportunity to use new vocabulary to reinforce their grasp of word meanings. Fourth, there is no substitute for the enthusiasm teachers can convey about the value of acquiring new vocabulary. Teachers can be effective models by using the words students are expected to learn.

A final principle of effective vocabulary instruction is eclecticism in teaching. Students learn in a variety of ways; therefore, successful vocabulary instruction calls for a repertoire of activities. For purposes of this book, prereading activities for helping students assimilate new vocabulary are divided between those that focus on helping students infer the meanings of words by the way they are used in a passage and those that emphasize categorization of words.

Inferring Word Meanings From Context

This section describes two teaching strategies—Contextual Redefinition and Possible Sentences—which emphasize context as an avenue to vocabulary development.

Contextual Redefinition

All human experience is dependent on context, a necessary and natural part of reading and comprehending. Many reading educators stress the importance of using context in verifying and interpreting the meanings of words which, in turn, leads to more effective processing of print. The use of context also allows readers to make informed guesses about the meaning of words in print and to monitor those guesses by checking them for accuracy as reading continues. In essence, context enables readers to predict a word's meaning by making connections between their prior knowledge and the text.

Frequently, writers provide various direct clues to the meanings of words in sentences. These clues might include the use of synonyms, a description or definition, familiar expressions, or comparison and contrast with other concepts. Although it might not be important for students to identify which type of context clue is provided, it is essential that they be able to use these devices to derive meaning. Contextual Redefinition (Moore, Moore, Cunningham, & Cunningham, 1998; Readence, Bean, & Baldwin, 1998), provides a format for students to realize the importance of context in ascertaining meaning.

To demonstrate the strategy, consider the words *vapid, lummox,* and *piebald.* Would you be able to provide a definition for these terms? If not, read the following sentences to see if they help.

1. Even though she intended to discuss a lively issue, her conversation with me was *vapid*, lacking animation and force.

2. As a result of his ungainly, slovenly appearance, Bill was often unjustly labeled a *lummox*.

3. Though described as *piebald* because of its spotted black and white colors, the horse was still considered beautiful by many horse lovers.

If you did not already know the meanings of the terms, the sentences probably were helpful in determining the meanings. Good readers use context, often subconsciously, as a clue to meaning. Many students who are not efficient readers do not effectively use context, particularly when they face new information in subject-matter textbooks. Teachers can greatly enhance students' ability to comprehend text by teaching them the use of context, instead of assuming they already use the strategy.

Contextual Redefinition involves the following steps:

1. *Select unfamiliar words.* Identify words students will encounter in text that are central to comprehending important concepts and that may present trouble for students as they read.

2. *Write a sentence.* Provide a context for each word with appropriate clues to the word's meaning. If such a context already exists, use it. In the examples presented with *vapid, lummox,* and *piebald,* clues of definition or description were provided.

3. *Present the words in isolation.* Using a transparency or chalkboard, ask students to provide a meaning for each word. Students defend their guesses and, as a group, come to some consensus as to the best definition. An accurate meaning may be offered, but many times the guesses might be humorous or even "off the wall"; this is part of the process of realizing the importance of context in vocabulary learning.

4. *Present the words in a sentence.* Using the sentence or short paragraph previously developed, present the word in its appropriate context. Again, students should be asked to offer guesses as to the meaning of each word and to defend their definitions. In this way less able readers will be able to experience the thinking processes involved in deriving a definition from context. In essence, students act as models of appropriate reading behavior for one another.

5. *Dictionary verification.* Students then consult a dictionary to verify the meaning.

It is important for teachers to remember to model their thinking in using context and to demonstrate the use of Contextual Redefinition before expecting students to use the strategy. It is also imperative to remember that Contextual Redefinition is a strategy that only introduces new vocabulary words. After reading and discussing the words in class, provide students postreading situations to broaden and reinforce their understanding of the words. Additional practice gives students more of an opportunity to retain newly learned words in long-term memory for later use.

Several benefits can be derived from the use of Contextual Redefinition. Students should realize that (1) simply guessing the meaning of a word in isolation is frustrating, haphazard, and probably not very accurate; (2) context provides clues to the meaning of words which allows informed guesses that may approximate dictionary definitions; and (3) motivation is necessary to discover the meaning of unknown words. Students have the potential to independently apply informed guessing through context in other forms of reading.

Contextual Redefinition also can be used to teach students to infer the meanings of words from their structure, in this case using the parts of words, *morphemes*, that have meaning in and of themselves. Morphemes are either free or bound. Free morphemes can function alone as a word, for example, *some* or *thing* in the word *something*. Bound morphemes are those meaningful language units that occur only as attachments to words or other morphemes, for example, *tele-*, which deals with distance, or *-ist*, which means "one who performs an action." In essence, these are prefixes, suffixes, or roots. Just as a word may be a symbol representing meaning in our knowledge structure, so may a word part or morpheme.

If a word that you want to introduce includes some known morphemes and you are using Contextual Redefinition, it might be useful to focus students' attention on those parts when presenting the word to them. This will enhance students' guesses and make them more informed. Additionally, it will expose students unfamiliar with morphemes with another way to get at meaning. Let us look at the word *matricide* in the following sentence: *Matricide was a form of sacrifice practiced in this ancient culture to appease their religious fervor.* Using Contextual Redefinition students would venture guesses as to the meaning of matricide, but clues by the teacher to think about the word parts might produce some close to accurate guesses that could be verified in context. If students knew *maternal* or *matron* and that these words are associated with motherhood, and/or homicide or suicide and that they are associated with killing, guesses about the target word would be more informed.

If you wish to focus on the morphemes a word may contain when using Contextual Redefinition, be sure that they are common ones and are not obscure. For instance, how important would it be for students to know that *arachi-*, in the word *arachibutyrophobia*, deals with peanuts when they may never encounter that morpheme again?

Possible Sentences

Possible Sentences (Moore & Moore, 1992) is a combination vocabulary/prediction activity designed to acquaint students with new vocabulary in their reading, guide them in verifying the accuracy of the statements they generate, and arouse curiosity concerning the passage to be read. Possible Sentences is best used when unfamiliar vocabulary is mixed with familiar terminology. This activity consists of five steps:

1. List key vocabulary
2. Elicit sentences
3. Read in order to verify sentences
4. Evaluate sentences
5. Generate new sentences

The following example text will be used to describe Possible Sentences. The length of this text is not typical of students' reading assignments but does serve to illustrate the strategy being discussed.

Warts Still Defy Spunk Water and More Scientific Cures

Utter medical humility certainly was displayed by dermatologists at the University of Cincinnati when they announced that after a 20-year study of warts, they were no nearer finding a satisfactory cure than when they started. Although the scientists concluded that the verrucae are produced by a polyoma virus, a highly contagious carrier, they confessed that they weren't really further advanced than Hippocrates in suggesting reasons for the incidence of warts, or nostrums for their cure. This leaves orthodox doctors with treatments such as caustic painting, freezing, or electro-cautery.

Warts tend to come and go at their own volition. Their evanescence has made them a target for old wives' charms and autosuggestive cures. And such folk medicine doesn't seem to have progressed any better over the decades than that of professional practitioners. Pliny the Elder, in the first century A.D., advised afflicted Romans to touch each of their nodules with a pea, wrap the peas in a cloth, and throw the parcel away behind them. The magical theory was the symbolic transference of evil in which the person picking up the package would pick up warts as well.

The popularity of Tom Sawyer has led to widespread reliance among rural and verrucose Americans on the character's prescription of sprinkling warts with "spunk water," rainwater scooped from a tree stump in the woods. Interestingly, spunk water never existed in the American language until Mark Twain dreamed it up (adapted from Ryan, 1977).

To determine the key vocabulary in this passage, the following concepts are selected as most important:

- Medical science has not been able to find a cure for warts.
- Current treatments consist of caustic painting, freezing, and electrocautery.
- Folk cures for warts have descended through the ages.

1. *List key vocabulary.* In order to lead students to the above concepts, list the following vocabulary on the chalkboard and pronounce each word as you write it.

Warts

dermatologists

verrucae

polyoma virus

nostrums

caustic painting

freezing

electrocautery

autosuggestive cures

Pliny the Elder

verrucose

spunk water

Mark Twain

2. *Elicit sentences.* Ask students to select at least two words from the list and formulate a sentence using the words. The resulting sentence must be one they think might be in the text. It is useful to model a possible sentence and the thinking required in formulating one. Record the sentences verbatim, even if the information is not correct, and underline the words used from the list. Students may use words already in sentences provided that a new context is created. Cease recording the sentences after a specified period of time, when all the words have been used, or when the students can produce no more. Following are some sentences that might be elicited using Possible Sentences.

   (a) *Freezing* and *electrocautery* are two methods *dermatologists* use to remove warts.

   (b) Three types of warts are *verrucae, nostrums,* and *verrucose.*

   (c) *Mark Twain* said to use *spunk water* to remove warts.

   (d) Three home remedies for removing warts are *spunk water, autosuggestive cures,* and *caustic painting.*

   (e) *Pliny the Elder* discovered the *polyoma virus.*

3. *Read to verify sentences.* Have students read the text selection for the explicit purpose of verifying the accuracy of their possible sentences.

4. *Evaluate sentences.* After the reading, have students evaluate each sentence. The text selection may be used as a reference. Evaluate sentences according to their accuracy, and refine or omit those that are inaccurate. Such discussion calls for careful reading, and judgments of the accuracy of the generated sentences must be defended. Thus, students model their thinking for one another. Examining the possible sentences listed earlier, sentences (a) and (c) may be accepted as they stand. Sentence (b) will have to be modified because *verrucae* is the only word listed in the sentence that is synonymous with warts. This sentence might be modified to the following: Verrucose people are constantly seeking *nostrums* for the cure of their *verrucae.* Sentence (d) can be modified by omitting *caustic painting* as a home cure because it is a remedy used by dermatologists. Finally, sentence (e) has to be modified because *Pliny the Elder* did not discover the *polyoma virus.* It could be modified as follows: *Pliny the Elder,* unaware that warts are caused by the *polyoma virus,* suggested a folk remedy for getting rid of warts.

5. *Generate new sentences.* After evaluation and modification of the original sentences are accomplished, ask students for new sentences. New sentences are generated with the intent of extending student understanding of the text concepts. As these sentences are dictated, have students check them for accuracy, using the text selection for confirmation. Students should record all final acceptable sentences in their notebooks.

Possible Sentences provides students an opportunity to practice their language skills, and is a proven strategy to teach vocabulary (Stahl & Kapinus, 1991). Using their prior knowledge, students think of and evaluate possible connections new vocabulary terms may have. They speak to express their associations and listen to others' thoughts and associations. They read to verify the possible combinations and discuss their findings in postreading situations. Finally, students use their newly gained content knowledge with their prior knowledge to practice other possible sentence combinations that will allow them to continue to extend and reinforce their meanings for the vocabulary terms.

Fading instruction with context. The purpose of using context as a learning strategy is to get students to make tentative predictions about the meanings of words using their prior knowledge and, subsequently, to use context independently as a means to verify their guesses. Demonstration by the teacher and guided practice for the students help students understand the process of using context to infer meaning. Merely telling students that using context when they read text assignments will be helpful in inferring meanings of unfamiliar words may not be enough.

Teachers need to explain context and model its use. After one or two demonstration sessions, guided practice should be provided with students using context repeatedly and with teacher feedback and reteaching when appropriate. Teachers provide sentences containing relevant unknown words and ask students to predict their meaning using the context. Students explain to the class how they used the context to arrive at a word's meaning, compare their explanations about how they used context, and receive feedback concerning accuracy from the teacher and other students.

Opportunities need to be provided for students to learn to use context on their own. Students in small groups are more apt to actively participate in the learning situation. The whole class could be used as a forum with the teacher providing feedback to the small groups on the accuracy of their use of context and the thinking involved. It is important to find out if students can verbalize how to use context. If they can, they probably can use context successfully on their own.

Fading can begin by having students work on their own before they meet in small groups. Differences in their predictions about meanings of words can be worked out in the small group before the teacher works with them in the large group. Next, students would work independently without the small group. Feedback would be given on their application of the strategy in the large group only. Finally, as a test of a true independent application of the strategy, feedback would not be given to the large group, and individual assistance would be provided only as needed. This emulates the type of situation students would be involved in if they were actually reading on their own. The only difference is that the teacher provides students the key words from the text; in true independent reading situations, students would have to decide the importance of words as they encounter them and use context to infer the meanings. The dictionary would remain the source for checking the accuracy of predicted word meanings.

Categorizing Words

Whether using Contextual Redefinition, Possible Sentences, or other strategies designed to introduce vocabulary, context serves as the vehicle for verifying tentative guesses about the meanings of unknown words. However, while determining meaning, context may not always reveal it (Schatz & Baldwin, 1986). Teachers need to clarify the meanings of important vocabulary terms. Although this may not seem desirable, we are not suggesting that telling students the meaning of unknown words means providing short definitions or synonyms for them. A study of words in this way is a very narrow approach to vocabulary development because it neglects important relationships that add depth to word meanings.

When we advise telling students the meanings of new vocabulary, we are advocating two systematic teaching strategies to develop concepts based on students' prior knowledge, specifically List-Group-Label and Feature Analysis. The expected learning outcome resulting from these strategies is that students will be able to use categorization as a means to understand new vocabulary and accompanying concepts.

List-Group-Label

The List-Group-Label lesson (also called Semantic Mapping) was originally conceived by Taba (1967) as a vocabulary development activity in social studies and science. It is based on the use of categorization as a way to teach students to organize their verbal concepts. Thus, List-Group-Label is most appropriate when many of the concepts are familiar so prior knowledge can be activated and connections made to the topic.

The lesson begins with the teacher supplying students with a stimulus topic drawn from their experiences or from the materials they are studying. Next, students develop a list of words they associate with the topic. A spiraling effect occurs; that is, initial associations with the topic promote more associations and connections by other students. The teacher records the associations until the list totals 25 to 30 words. The students then construct smaller lists of words from the large list and provide a label for each grouping. Approximately three to five words are placed in the smaller groups, and students then explain why they have grouped words in a particular manner.

When used as a prereading strategy, the List-Group-Label lesson is designed to activate students' content knowledge, thereby enhancing comprehension. To exemplify its use as a prereading activity in the content areas, the stimulus topic geometry will be demonstrated as used in a seventh-grade math class. The students were briefly introduced to geometry in sixth grade, but the seventh-grade curriculum called for a lengthier study. The students generated the following list of words.

Geometry

square	rectangle
cubic centimeters	triangular prism
math	base
volume	side
area	cylinder
cube	prism
pyramid	face
cone	edge
sphere	corner
symmetry	congruence
ruler	surface
protractor	compass
square inches	circle
equilateral	triangle

The students next made smaller groups of words from the list and labeled them. Following are examples of these groups.

Geometry Groups

- Protractor, ruler, compass = measurement tools
- Sphere, cone, circle, cylinder = curved surfaces
- Square inches, volume, area, cubic centimeters = forms of measurements
- Cylinder, prism, cube, pyramid, square = things that have faces
- Prism, cone, cube, triangular prism = space figures
- Square, sphere, corner, volume, circle = words with six letters
- Side, symmetry, square, square inches, surface = words beginning with *s*

As can be seen, the majority of the word groups are based on meaningful, semantic associations. However, the last two groups are based on surface-level spelling cues rather than semantic cues. This is not the desired outcome of the List-Group-Label lesson even though such associations might serve as important mnemonic devices for some students as they deal with the text material. The purpose of this lesson is to stimulate meaningful word associations, thereby activating students' prior knowledge.

The List-Group-Label lesson also may be used as a follow-up activity in the postreading stage of a content area lesson. The steps are identical, but the purpose is different. In the postreading stage, this strategy is used for review and reinforcement of text concepts; that is, students are encouraged to use the content knowledge they have gained from the text in addition to related prior knowledge to form groups and label them. The List-Group-Label lesson also helps teachers ascertain whether students have learned the important text concepts.

Feature Analysis

Feature Analysis is intended to provide students with a systematic teaching procedure for exploring, reinforcing, and organizing vocabulary concepts through categorization (Pittelman, Heimlich, Berglund, & French, 1991). This strategy is somewhat complex and should be used with relatively sophisticated middle and secondary school students.

Feature Analysis is composed of the following steps:

1. *Category selection.* It is best to begin this strategy with a text topic familiar to the students. Once acquainted with Feature Analysis, categories may become less well known. *Planets of the solar system* will be the category used here.

2. *List category terms.* The teacher provides terms for concepts or objects connected to the category topic. These terms can be provided by students once they are accustomed to the strategy. In the case of our category, the following planet names might be introduced: *Mercury, Venus, Earth,* and *Mars.*

3. *List features.* You and your students must now decide which features to explore. It is best to start with a few features and add more later in the lesson. For instance, features to be examined are whether the planets are hot, cold, big, small, and life-supporting. After these steps have been completed, the following feature matrix should result.

Planets

	hot	cold	big	small	life
Mercury					
Venus					
Earth					
Mars					

4. *Indicate feature possession.* Students are guided through the feature matrix for the purpose of deciding whether a particular planet possesses each of the features. Teachers should first demonstrate how to deal with the matrix by modeling their thinking. It is recommended that a simple plus/minus (+/-) system be used initially to indicate feature possession. Later, a more sophisticated system such as a Likert scale (1 = always, 2 = some, 3 = never) may be used when students become familiar with Feature Analysis and want to explore the relative degree of feature possession. Feature possession should be based on typical patterns; that is, a plus sign indicates that a category item usually has the feature. The presence of the same sign in opposite features can indicate a third feature, that is, if a planet is neither big nor small, it is medium sized. Through demonstration and guided practice, the feature matrix for planets should look like the following, using a +/- system.

Planets

	hot	cold	big	small	life
Mercury	+	-	-	+	-
Venus	+	-	-	-	-
Earth	-	-	-	-	+
Mars	-	-	-	+	-

5. *Add terms/features.* The matrix should be expanded by adding new terms to be explored—in this case, the rest of the planets—and new features to be analyzed—in this case, the presence of *rings* and *moons.* Students can generate these items in an attempt to further expand their knowledge of the topic. (This step can be eliminated once students are familiar with, and motivated to use, the strategy by using all terms and features in the initial matrix.)

6. *Complete and explore matrix.* The final step is to complete the expanded matrix and form generalizations about the category terms. The completed matrix should look like the following.

Planets

	hot	cold	big	small	life	rings	moons
Mercury	+	-	-	+	-	-	-
Venus	+	-	-	-	-	-	-
Earth	-	-	-	-	+	-	+
Mars	-	-	-	+	-	-	+
Jupiter	-	+	+	-	-	+	+
Saturn	-	+	+	-	-	+	+
Uranus	-	+	+	-	-	+	+
Neptune	-	+	+	-	-	-	+
Pluto	-	+	-	+	-	-	-

The class explores the matrix after it is completed. This entails students examining how the terms (planets) are similar, yet unique. You can demonstrate this by noting that although the Earth shares a number of characteristics with other planets, it is the only planet that is life supporting. Later, you can ask questions to motivate students' observations. Finally, have students make their own connections by noting similarities and differences. Some questions you could ask students are, Which planets are the coldest? Which have moons? How is Pluto different from Mars? What makes Earth a unique planet? Which planet is most like Earth? Why? As students interact, divergent comments and changes in the matrix are welcome as long as their reasoning is sound. When the exploration is completed, direct students to read the text to verify their categorizations.

Postreading activities with Feature Analysis revolve around a discussion of the accuracy of the categorization in prereading. Corrections are made if support from the text is cited. Additionally, students can further expand the matrix by adding text knowledge they have picked up while reading. The final corrected and expanded feature matrix is then copied into students' notebooks as additional reinforcement and a source for study.

Fading instruction with categorization. The purpose of categorization is to help students develop their vocabulary by attending to relationships among words. The ultimate goal of categorization is to teach students to apply it independently in their reading assignments. However, because the categorization strategies are teacher directed and may be based on information for which students have little prior knowledge, categorization does not lend itself to fading as well as strategies that utilize context.

Nevertheless, teachers can progressively withdraw their involvement in these learning situations by using a technique of moving from a whole group to a small group to an individual format as students become accustomed to using categorization. Small groups can provide an effective format for students to collaboratively use categorization as a means of developing their content knowledge. Students who possess extensive prior knowledge of a particular topic may be able to independently brainstorm their own categories related to a topic under study in prereading. Then these students can be directed to read to verify their categories and expand them in postreading. For those students, categorization can serve as an independent study aid when the teacher is not available for feedback.

Summary

This chapter has presented a rationale for introducing text vocabulary and principles essential to effective vocabulary development. Four teaching strategies have been presented to aid teachers in developing students' vocabularies. Contextual Redefinition can be used when a few words can be defined by the context in which they occur. Possible Sentences is appropriate when unfamiliar vocabulary is mixed with familiar terminology so students can attempt to associate new information with known information. When context does not work, two activities can be used for teaching new vocabulary using concept development models—List-Group-Label and Feature Analysis.

The importance of such direct instruction in vocabulary development cannot be overemphasized. Additionally, using strategies that involve students in discovering the meaning of new words and provide a potential format for independent learning are essential.

Chapter 5

Graphically Representing Information

PURPOSE

This chapter demonstrates the effectiveness of previewing information to be learned in a passage using a graphic representation, allowing students to see how concepts are related within the context of a chapter of text or unit of study.

Strategies

I. The *Semantic Web* allows students to note the relationships among concepts presented in the text.

2. The *Graphic Organizer* presents a schematic diagram of major concepts and additional terms that convey the text structure to students before reading.

3. The *Outline* organizes major concepts and pertinent details in a hierarchical organization.

4. The *Word Map* visually depicts the definition of a word and the concept the word represents, including primary properties of the word and examples.

5. *K-W-L* provides a framework for students to activate their background knowledge and set independent purposes prior to learning about a topic they are going to be studying.

6. *I-Charts*, also known as Inquiry Charts, allow students to access, compare and contrast, and integrate information from multiple sources.

7. *Talking Drawings* allow readers to transform background information into simple drawings that become the focus for discussion and learning.

Graphic representations of information depict relationships among concepts so that students have a map of an upcoming passage or unit lesson. Just as maps are useful for travelers wishing to reach a desired location without getting lost, graphic representations of text can allow readers to navigate their way through what they read. Webbing, Graphic Organizers, and Outlines depict the organization of textual material, enabling students to be guided through information that is important to learn and remember. The Word Map explores nuances of word meanings, delving much deeper than traditional vocabulary instruction and graphically analyzing the meanings. K-W-L, I-Charts, and Talking Drawings give teachers the means to activate students' background knowledge prior to reading and engage in higher level thinking activities that promote the understanding of material beyond the literal level. Graphically representing information through these techniques provides students with a framework for previewing and reading a passage. Students learn to anticipate expected learning outcomes (see Chapter 1). Also, as discussed in Chapter 3, these expectations can form the basis for making judgments while reading that can directly enhance comprehension. In this way, information can be assimilated more readily than if students are thrust into a passage with no preparation other than being told to "Read Chapter 9 for tomorrow. Be ready to discuss it."

The positive effects of graphically representing text can be explained by schema theory. A schema is a framework for how individuals view the world and is tied closely to prior knowledge. This framework forms the basis for integrating new information. Schemata also represent individual beliefs and perceptions. Because new information being processed must filter through these schemata in some way, being able to activate prior knowledge is essential before new information can be integrated into long-term memory. The quality and quantity of new information learned, therefore, are related closely to the quality and quantity of what is already known, that is, schemata/prior knowledge.

Research (e.g., Beck, Omanson, & McKeown, 1982) has established that comprehension can be enhanced by identifying the instructional framework of a text and giving students the tools necessary for structuring that information. For example, expository text is structured in a factual, objective way. On the other hand, literary text usually engages students' interests by drawing them into a story. Students who can identify the differences between these structures can more easily form expectations on which to base their reading predictions. Graphic depictions of text structure enable students to become familiar with this structure while reading, allowing them to become independent readers, learners, and thinkers.

The following strategies allow students to observe and learn methods for structuring new information so it can be more readily understood and give students experiences with text and the structure of textual concepts so they may individually acquire reading and thinking strategies.

Semantic Web

The Semantic Web is a lesson-based or unit-based strategy for visually graphing the structure of the text to define and show important relationships among major concepts to be presented. Webs can be constructed for different sections of a text, depending on how in-depth the focus of the study will be. For instance, with younger students, a Web can be constructed for a paragraph from a unit of study. In this case, almost all main ideas and details can be integrated into the Web. This may work well for a paragraph that has a large number of important concepts that are traditionally difficult for students to comprehend. Older students may construct a Web for an entire chapter of content text. In this case, many details will be omitted for the sake of convenience, and only ideas that directly support the main ideas will be included. This forces students to pay attention to details, including in the Web only those elements essential to the overall understanding of the text. It also allows students to focus on any central questions that may have been posed for the unit. The center of the Web contains the main idea(s), and the spokes contain related information. The shape of the Web is determined by the text being studied. There is no standard format that all Webs follow. Different types of text would dictate different types of structures. (A Web for a chapter in a social studies text introducing the state of Pennsylvania might look like Figure 1.) The following are steps for constructing a Web.

1. *Draw a circle for the center of the Web.* This circle should be larger than all others and be heavily outlined to show that it is the hub around which all the other ideas emanate.

2. *Write the main idea from the paragraph, page, or chapter in the center of the circle.* This should be one or two words that best summarize the main idea. This also should be written in bold letters to draw attention to it.

Figure 1
Web on Pennsylvania

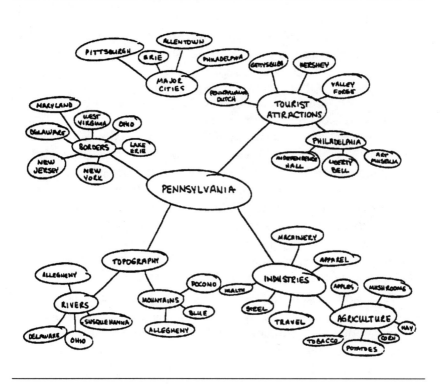

3. *List supporting information related to the main idea.* Students should brainstorm ideas for several minutes, listing words related to the key word or phrase. These ideas should be written on the chalkboard for future reference.

4. *Create the Web by placing key words or phrases on new spokes until ideas are exhausted.* Information that is directly related to the main idea should be identified and listed in smaller circles at the end of spokes emanating from the center circle. Next, words or phrases that relate to the main ideas are identified from the brainstormed list. These words are written at the end of the spokes. It is important to note that word spokes also can emanate from details to which they are related. Thus, an idea may be two or more spokes away from the center of the Web.

5. *The class explores and discusses the Web, adding, deleting, or modifying ideas as needed.* During this step, students can compare their own prior knowledge to the structure of the Web, become aware of new words, and relate new words and knowledge to those that are already known. Through class discussion, the teacher can assess an individual student's abilities in order to make instructional decisions.

Webs for fictional stories can be constructed from basal readers or from literature studies in language arts and English. These Webs would depict elements of the story and give students practice in identifying story structure. Webs can be employed effectively during prereading to focus students' attention on the main ideas, vocabulary, and structure of the text. Because brainstorming a story with which students are unfamiliar is difficult, the teacher could use the opportunity to provide the students with main idea and detail terms before reading. As students read or study the lesson, they try to create a Web that places the terms in a structure that makes sense to them. These individual Webs then could be used to promote postreading class discussions.

Webs can be used after reading to review the major ideas and their relationships presented in a lesson. The teacher provides the major topics, and students fill in related details from the text during and after reading. In another related activity, the teacher provides an incomplete Web with some of the words filled in. From a list provided by the teacher, students fill in the remaining terms to construct a Web that fits the ideas into a structure that makes sense.

Webs also can be used independently by students. The teacher can demonstrate how main ideas and details from text fit together. These can be discussed before a chapter is read, allowing students to use the teacher-made Web during reading to help connect information. Guided practice would involve students in completing Web templates started by the teacher but with some information missing. As students read, they are charged with supplying the missing information. A follow-up class discussion can weigh students' copies as good or poor choices, keeping in mind that Webs need not be identical. A key to fading instruction is that students must be made aware of the advantages of using a Web. Through demonstration and small-group practice students can become more adept at this task. With teacher motivation students can use Webs independently for study aids for tests and other related classroom activities.

Graphic Organizer

The Graphic Organizer (Barron & Earle, 1973), also known as the structured overview, presents a schematic diagram for major concepts and additional terms that convey information to students before they read. This lesson- or unit-based strategy has been used primarily with secondary students, but it can be used successfully with students in the earlier grades. It also can be easily adapted to many content areas. Tierney and Readence (2000) explain how a Graphic Organizer can be used as a point of reference when students begin to read and study in detail. Used as a unit-based strategy, students may focus on the central question of the unit. Following are steps used in the construction of a Graphic Organizer.

1. *The teacher identifies the major objectives and concepts to be taught.* The following concepts and terms were identified from a chapter on "Fibers" in *Steps in Clothing Skill* (Draper & Bailey, 1978), which could be used in a secondary home economics class.

Key Concepts

- Fibers can be either natural or man-made.
- Natural fibers can be obtained from animals or vegetables; man-made fibers are chemically produced.
- Examples of natural fibers include cotton, linen, wool, and silk.
- Examples of man-made fibers include acrylic, rayon, nylon, polyester, and acetate.

Key Terms

fibers	acrylic	silkworm
yarn	nylon	cocoon
fabric	acetate	man-made fibers
cotton	linen	rayon
flax	wool	polyester

2. *The key terms are arranged into a diagram that parallels the text structure, stressing relationships between and among terms.* Depicting text relationships may be considered to be one advantage of a Graphic Organizer over an outline. The structure can take many forms, although coordinate terms should be at parallel levels. Notice that this is different from Webs, where the terms sur-

Figure 2
Graphic Organizer on Fibers

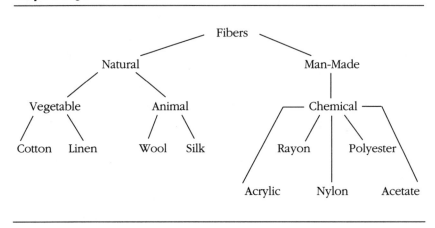

round the main ideas, and coordinate terms may be at different places around the wheel. Terms may be deleted or others added from the previous list in order to make the organizer more coherent. You should consider the students' background of information and the organization of the text when constructing the organizer. Figure 2 shows a diagram that would be appropriate for the chapter on fibers. Different diagrams could be drawn for the same passage to determine the best fit for different groups of students, based on ability and prior knowledge.

3. *Present the Graphic Organizer to the class.* A chalkboard can be used to present the Organizer to the students, but an overhead projector is recommended. Present the diagram to the students little by little by using a piece of paper on top of the transparency. Talk the students through the diagram, explaining any unclear relationships and encouraging discussion of key points. Each section is presented and discussed until the entire diagram has been displayed. After discussion, the diagram can be left in place for use as a reference during silent reading and subsequent discussion.

The Graphic Organizer can be a powerful tool for helping students. If a reader wonders how the author jumped from topic A to topic B, a quick glance at the Graphic Organizer can resolve the uncertainties.

A Graphic Organizer often can be made to reflect the text structure of the author. Knowledge of the structure of a text in making predictions for reading is extremely important. A well-organized text will demand less of a student's attention while reading than a poorly structured text (Readence, Bean, & Baldwin, 1998).

A Graphic Organizer can be used by students when surveying a text (see Chapter 2). An incomplete diagram is displayed, and students are told which text pattern of organization the author has used. The students survey the chapter in order to fill in the missing sections of the organizer.

As with Webs, an incomplete diagram can be used after the students have read a passage using a Graphic Organizer. The same diagram used to enhance readiness in the prereading stage also can be used to aid in the recall of material after reading. For instance, blanks can be left in the original diagram for students to fill in by recalling the organization of the new text material learned during silent reading. Deleted words are listed in random order under the diagram. Figure 3 shows a Graphic Post-Organizer for the "fibers" example.

Students either recall or locate appropriate terms and concepts in order to complete the diagram. This form can be put on a handout

Figure 3
Graphic Post-Organizer for Fibers

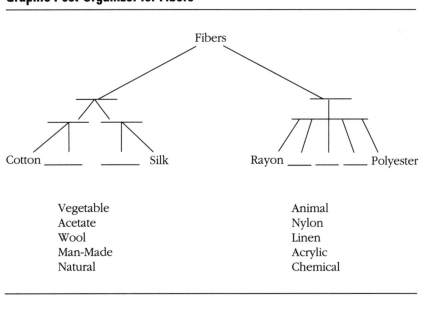

and used as a quiz or as a study aid for a test. In an analysis of past Graphic Organizer research, Moore and Readence (1984) found it advantageous to ask students to construct Graphic Organizers after reading, especially when vocabulary words were used in the graphic. This lends support to the practice of using Graphic Organizers as a postreading activity.

Fading from teacher to student control is difficult with the Graphic Organizer because prior knowledge of the topic is necessary. It would be quite easy for a teacher to model the use of a Graphic Organizer, but guided practice and independent use would be more difficult. If extended into a reading and postreading activity, fading can be accomplished as students become familiar with text patterns and the Graphic Organizer. After the teacher introduces the concept of Graphic Organizers and students master the skills necessary for their construction, students can be encouraged to survey text chapters independently and produce original diagrams. Students can refine these rough Graphic Organizers as they read by adding, deleting, or modifying the original diagrams. The diagrams can be compared in small groups, with students defending their reasoning for choices made. Students can use the modified versions of their Graphic Organizers as study guides. Again, caution students that there is no correct construction as long as the Graphic Organizer adequately depicts the development and relationships between major concepts.

Outline

Outlining skills have been taught for years. The Outline is similar to the Web and the Graphic Organizer in that major concepts and pertinent details are identified; the difference is in how the information is represented graphically. In the Web, information radiates in spokes outward from the major topic. The Graphic Organizer presents coordinate terms in a parallel structure. In an Outline, information is organized hierarchically. This lesson- or unit-based strategy is often used with content material to impose a written structure on term papers, organize class lecture notes, study for a test, and pursue answers to central questions.

Research (e.g., Glynn & DiVesta, 1977) indicates that Outlines presented before a reading task facilitate student comprehension; that is, factual recall can be improved significantly when Outlines are used as a prereading technique to familiarize students with new material. Outlining can be an efficient vehicle for promoting learning when used before the information is presented in text and when teachers maintain responsibility for its construction. An example of an Outline that could be used for the topic on fibers might look like the following:

Fibers
    I. Natural
            A. Vegetable
                    1. Cotton
                    2. Linen
            B. Animal
                    1. Wool
                    2. Silk

    II. Man-made
            A. Chemical
                    1. Acrylic
                    2. Rayon
                    3. Nylon
                    4. Polyester
                    5. Acetate

In presenting the Outline to a class, you could use an overhead projector with a sheet of paper as a mask. As each new element of the Outline is uncovered, clarify unclear points and encourage discussion to assess prior knowledge. The organization of the text will become apparent through the gradual building of the text structure in Outline form.

The use of Outlines should be restricted to texts arranged in an ordered format where general concepts are sequentially introduced and supported with appropriate detail. Texts that do not follow such an organized format would be poor candidates for this strategy. When the text is organized loosely, a Graphic Organizer probably would be more useful.

An incomplete diagram can be used with the Outline, with students relying on headings and subheadings in the text to fill in the incomplete form. Students follow the sequential development of the text to decide which terms fit the blanks. Unlike the Graphic Organizer, only a limited number of terms properly fit each blank because of the more organized text format.

In fading outlining instruction, it is important that the concept of outlining be understood before independent practice takes place. Many students successfully complete Outline workbook exercises without really understanding what an Outline is. Identifying main idea, topic and subtopic, and details and subdetails is crucial to fading instruction, as is the ability to identify texts that do not lend themselves to the Outline format. Students must realize that outlining cannot be done effectively with all texts. Through modeling, teachers can provide examples to students based on information being studied.

Word Map

A Word Map is a graphic representation of the definition of a word. It is based on the notion that before students can say what a word means, they must have developed a *concept of definition* (Schwartz & Raphael, 1985). They must have the ability to identify and define new terms on their own, using prior knowledge and context clues. This lesson-based or unit-based strategy is ideal for moving students away from traditional teacher-directed vocabulary lessons toward independence. It is useful in all content areas for students at all levels of instruction and allows students to deal with central questions posed for a unit.

When students are told to use the context to figure out the meaning of an unknown word, they often do not understand exactly what is meant. They may understand that context means the surrounding words and sentences without knowing exactly where they can find the information they need, because each example is unique. Often students do not realize that they have prior knowledge that may help them define an unknown word.

Schwartz and Raphael (1985) outlined the steps needed to teach students how to use Word Maps to define unknown words. Three categories of word relationships are used in Word Maps: (1) the general class to which a word belongs (What is it?); (2) the important properties of the word including those that distinguish it from members of its class (What is it like?); and (3) examples of the concept (What are some examples?). Word Maps usually work better with nouns but can be used with action verbs and other parts of speech. An example of a Word Map structure is shown in Figure 4.

In the center of the map, in the largest square, the concept being studied is written. Then, a general word or short phrase describing the word is written in the square at the top. This word is often the name of a generic class to which the word belongs. For instance, if *bear* is the concept being studied, a good word for the top square would be *mammal*. Next, the student answers the question, What is it like?, with words that fit the same category as the center word, for example, *lion, ele-*

Figure 4
Word Map for Bear

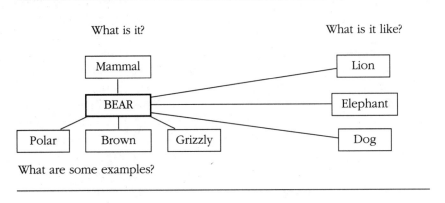

phant, and *dog*. It is important for these words to be at the same hierarchical level as the word being studied. For example, *animal* would be a poor choice because it is a broader term than bear. *Dalmatian* would be a poor choice because it is a specific breed of dog and not a generic mammal. Finally, examples of the concept are written in the bottom squares. *Polar*, *brown*, and *grizzly* are examples of bears.

Begin teaching Word Mapping to students by direct instruction through modeling. Students should learn the importance of figuring out unknown words while reading. Teachers can provide students with the motivation and enthusiasm for wanting to learn the meanings of new words. A strategy such as Contextual Redefinition (outlined in Chapter 4) can lead students into a discussion of the importance of knowing methods for gaining new word meanings. The Word Map can be shown on an overhead transparency or chalkboard, and concepts known to students can be mapped. By using familiar examples, students gain valuable practice in understanding the categories of questions used.

After students are familiar with the general format of Word Maps, you can construct independent exercises in which concepts are introduced in a rich context and all the information needed to fill in the map is in the text being read. At this level of guided practice, students gain practice in identifying unknown words and in getting the information needed to fill in the map from context.

After students master this step, use examples that gradually limit the information students will find. At this step, encourage students to use reference materials to locate information needed. Encyclopedias, almanacs, atlases, and alternate texts can help students. It is important to have plenty of sources available for students to use in the classroom, because several students may be looking up word concepts at the same time. Fading instruction is complete when students can internalize the questions from the Word Map, giving definitions of words without going through the mapping procedure. As students come across important unfamiliar terms while reading independently, they should ask themselves, "What is this word? What is it like? What are some examples of the word?" Students can revert to using the Map individually, if needed, on words particularly difficult to understand.

Word Maps have two advantages over some other methods of teaching students to understand the meanings of unknown words and concepts. First, by using the mapping technique (whether physically mapping the word or self-questioning about it), students gain more exposure to the word than simply looking up the meaning in the dictionary. This increases the chances that the word will be identified and defined at a later date. Second, Word Mapping promotes independent learning. The concept of fading instruction is built in, as the teacher instructs, provides examples, and practices the strategy with students. Because the steps in Word Mapping are clear, the activity should eliminate the uncertainty many students have during traditional vocabulary instruction related to basal and content text.

K-W-L

Since its introduction, K-W-L (Ogle, 1986) has become a very popular prereading strategy. Its implementation takes place in three steps. Students use a K-W-L chart, or strategy sheet, to first list what they *K*now about a topic that is going to be studied in the classroom. Then they list information in the chart that they *W*ant to find out about the topic. Finally, at the conclusion of the lesson, they add information that they *L*earned about the topic.

This lesson- or unit-based strategy is based on the notion that, as students brainstorm information that they might already know about a topic, they are activating the background knowledge they already have, greatly increasing the chances that they will integrate new knowledge with previously learned information. By listing what they want to learn, students are independently setting goals and purposes for reading and learning. In turn, this should increase their motivation as they search for answers to these questions. Finally, as they list what they have learned after reading, they are practicing summary writing skills, which enhance the comprehension process. As a unit-based strategy, K-W-L allows students to focus on any central questions that may be posed.

In order to carry out a K-W-L lesson, each student should have a blank copy of the strategy sheet. This sheet has three columns, one for each of the three categories outlined in its title. Assign students the topic that is going to be studied and ask them to fill in what they already know under the *K* column. For instance, if students are going to be studying *hurricanes*, their strategy sheet might look something like the following:

K	W	L
Powerful winds/rain		
Flooding		
Named after people		
Lots of damage		

At this point, you might have a short classroom discussion, allowing the students to share their brainstormed knowledge. This discussion is helpful because it allows the students additional opportunities to remember previously learned information. It also allows you to monitor student recalls to ensure that what students remember is accurate. After students have made a list of everything they remember about the topic, they then move to the *W* column and make a list of questions they want to learn about the topic. These questions can be based on the brainstormed information from the first step. Extending the hurricane example, the list might now look like this:

K	W	L
Powerful winds/rain	How do they form?	
Flooding	Where do they form?	
Named after people	When do they occur?	
Lots of damage	What are the most famous ones?	

As students read and learn information related to hurricanes, they will focus on the answers to these questions. Once they have finished reading about hurricanes, they fill in the *L* column, where they will list the answers to the previously generated question, plus add any other information that they found interesting. A completed K-W-L chart on the hurricane lesson might look like this:

K	W	L
Powerful winds/rain Flooding	How do they form?	Warm water meets jetstream air
	Where do they form?	Coast of Western Africa
Named after people Lots of damage	When do they occur? What are the most famous ones?	June-November Camille, Andrew, Hugo Must have winds of 74 mph or more

After students have completed the K-W-L chart, they can engage in regular postreading discussions, focusing on the questions and related answers from their sheets. If a question is not answered in the text, you might ask the student to locate it in another source. Teachers can eventually fade instruction so students can use K-W-L charts independently, allowing them to pursue individual lines of questioning while going beyond what is presented by the teacher and the author.

There have been several modifications to the K-W-L strategy, including K-W-L Plus (Carr & Ogle, 1987), in which students categorize and map the information they learn, and a strategy for combining focus questions into a K-W-L format (Huffman, 1998).

I-Chart

The Inquiry Chart strategy, commonly called I-Chart (Hoffman, 1992), builds on the K-W-L strategy. The goal of the unit-based I-Chart lesson is to build students' critical thinking skills by comparing and contrasting information from a number of different resources. Additionally, it allows students to study consistent and inconsistent information across reference sources in order to judge what information is accurate. When students are limited to only one reference source, they tend to assume that all the information presented is accurate. I-Charts encourage students to go beyond the page, to verify resources for accuracy, and to base factual learning on consistent information. I-Charts also allow students to pursue a unit's central questions.

Hoffman identified three phases to be used in an I-Chart lesson. Each phase contains several activities for implementing the procedure.

First Phase—Planning

1. *Topic identification:* Identify the topic that is to be studied. This strategy should work with most topics at any grade level, although Tierney and Readence (2000) suggest that it works best with students in the upper elementary grades and above.

2. *Question formation:* Formulate two to four questions linked to the major concepts you expect students to understand when learning about the topic.

3. *I-Chart construction:* An I-Chart is constructed based on the questions from Step 2. The chart might be quite large, so butcher paper or newsprint taped to a wall in the classroom tends to work best. List the topic of study in the upper left corner of the chart, and record the questions from Step 2 across the top row. A sample I-Chart is shown in Figure 5.

4. *Materials collection:* Collect materials that contain information on the topic to be studied. A variety of materials is important. For example, textbooks could be used, as well as encyclopedias, almanacs, newspapers and magazines, and trade books. The bibliographic information for each of these sources should be listed in the left column, and each reference should be listed in a different row.

Figure 5
Example of an I-Chart

		Guiding Questions					
	Topic	1.	2.	3.	4.	Interesting Facts and Figures	New Questions
	What We Know						
Sources	1.						
	2.						
	3.						
	Summary						

Second Phase—Interacting

In this phase, the students work along with the teacher to begin to fill in the I-Chart based on their background information. Students are encouraged to share interesting facts and generate new questions that come to mind as the discussion progresses.

1. *Exploration of prior knowledge and beliefs*: Probe the students to think about what they already know about the questions listed across the top row. Students may recall correct or incorrect information, but all recalls are accepted at this stage. This information is recorded in the boxes under the appropriate question, across the row labeled, "What We Know."

2. *Sharing of interesting facts and new questions*: You or your students record interesting facts that come up during the discussion in the box under the title, "Interesting Facts and Figures." The box to the right is used for students to list new questions they develop beyond those you posed. Questions can be added as they arise during the entire lesson.

3. *Reading and recording*: Students now consult the different reference sources to locate information related to questions in the chart. Information is entered into the appropriate box as accurately as possible. They might even want to list direct quotes from a source, if applicable. Students also can look for information related to the questions they recorded in the last column. The numbers of references and questions will dictate the size of the I-Chart. If many reference sources or questions are used, the chart can become quite large.

Third Phase—Integrating and Evaluating

During this final phase, the class can explore information in the chart by summarizing, comparing and contrasting, researching, and making conclusions about the information learned.

1. *Summarizing*: Ask students to write a summary statement for each question, based on what they learned from each source. In this process, students must synthesize and verify information to come up with a sentence that integrates information from all sources.

2. *Comparing*: Encourage students to compare their original background information, recorded in the "What We Know" column,

with the summary statements generated in the previous step. Inaccuracies can be noted and corrected.

3. *Researching*: New questions that are still unanswered should be assigned to students for further research. These questions can be assigned to individuals or groups of students who can then discuss their findings before adding answers to the chart.

4. *Reporting*: The students or groups of students report their findings to the class.

I-Charts provide an organized framework for students to learn and explore new information related to the classroom curriculum. The teacher could begin using I-Charts by leading students through each phase, being an integral part of the process. As students become familiar with this strategy, teacher involvement can be withdrawn gradually so that students can finally explore a topic either independently or in small groups with minimal teacher input. This process should help students learn critical thinking skills related to future research projects (Randall, 1996).

Talking Drawings

Talking Drawings (McConnell, 1992/1993) is a lesson-based prereading strategy that uses simple student drawings as a bridge between background knowledge and new information to be studied in the text. Teachers often begin a lesson by asking students to discuss what they already know about a topic in order to assess their knowledge base. This strategy offers an interesting twist by asking students to make a drawing showing what they already know about a topic. The following steps are involved in a Talking Drawings lesson:

1. Each student receives a piece of paper on which he or she is asked to draw a picture showing what is already known about the topic that is going to be studied. The drawing should be simple— a line drawing is fine—but should include as much detail as possible. For instance, the drawing in Figure 6 on page 80, centered on the topic of global warming, demonstrates that this student probably heard about the topic; however, because the drawing is quite simple, the student probably has little background knowledge about the causes and effects of global warming.

2. Students should get into small groups and share their drawings with the group, discussing the similarities and differences among the drawings.

3. A whole-class follow-up discussion takes place in which student groups discuss what they know about the topic and how they learned about it. The class then organizes their thoughts into a concept map. The teacher's role is that of a facilitator, with students taking the lead in the discussion.

4. Students are given a reading assignment related to the topic.

5. After a discussion about the reading, ask students to modify their previous drawings or begin a new drawing, based on what they have just learned. They are encouraged to add details reflecting the new information. Figure 7 shows a modified talking drawing.

6. The students then get into small groups again to compare and contrast their first and second drawings, focusing on what changes they made and what they learned about the topic that lead them to the change. Encourage them to refer to the reading assignment to clarify ideas. In the example, the second drawing contains much more information than the first and shows that the student is making the link between global warming and the melting ice caps.

Figure 6
Talking Drawing—First Attempt

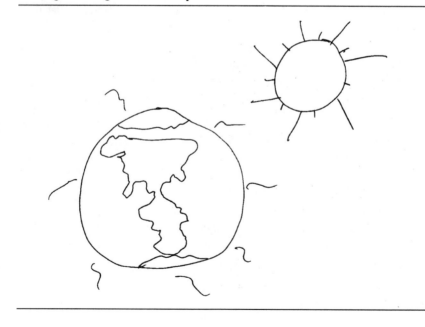

Figure 7
Talking Drawing—Second Attempt

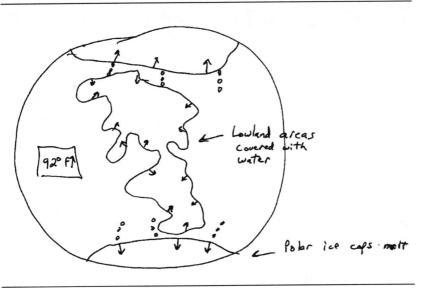

7. As an optional follow-up, you can assign students independent research to further their learning related to the topic.

McConnell (1992/1993) suggested that Talking Drawings can be used not only to introduce students to a topic prior to reading but also can be used to promote classroom discussion in a variety of subject areas and grade levels, including adult literacy programs.

Summary

This chapter has presented a rationale for graphically representing information in order to maximize student interaction with text. Several strategies have been presented that allow teachers to provide students with the tools for enhancing comprehension and promoting independent learning. These strategies can be used effectively before, during, and after reading to allow students to organize the information for reading and study. Suggestions for moving through the cycles of instruction with these strategies by fading control from the teacher to the students also have been discussed.

Chapter 6

Writing Before Reading

PURPOSE

Writing before reading promotes learning in a manner similar to the other strategies presented in this book. A special value of writing is that it provides a permanent record of thoughts.

Strategies

1. *Identification With a Story Character* begins with students writing about a situation similar to one a story character experiences.

2. The *Guided Writing Procedure* calls for students to brainstorm and categorize words related to a topic of study, use those words when writing about the topic, and then read a related passage.

3. The *Hennings Sequence* prepares students for writing in a manner similar to the Guided Writing Procedure, but this strategy details additional ways to help students draft the information they generate.

4. *Free Writing* involves a stream-of-consciousness recording of what students know about a topic.

5. *Quick Writes* allows students to use writing to anticipate what is to be learned in a lesson or review previous learning before new material is encountered.

Writing about a topic provides students opportunities to enhance their learning. Students who record their thoughts on paper frequently gain understandings that might be missed and retain understandings that might be forgotten. The effect of writing on learning received unprecedented attention by researchers and theorists during the 1970s and early 1980s, and much was published about writing in the content areas (Dyson & Freedman, 1991; Tierney & Shanahan, 1991).

The emphasis in this chapter differs from the emphases of most books and articles on writing. Here we focus on writing as a prereading strategy, with emphasis on increasing students' learning from text.

We suggest having students write what they know about a topic before reading about it to maximize reading comprehension and retention. The general rationale of writing before reading matches the rationale of the other prereading strategies presented in this book. Writing before reading is especially useful for increasing motivation by stimulating students' curiosity, activating students' prior knowledge, and focusing students' attention on important information.

Along with these outcomes, writing seems to improve learning from text because it provides a permanent record of thoughts. Writers use the permanence of paper, chalkboards, and computers to hold their words in place. With a record of their thoughts permanently stored, writers are able to examine and refine their thinking. Careful review and revision of one's thoughts are possible when a written record is available.

The permanence of writing can be exploited before reading so that learners produce a complete, well-defined statement of what they do and do not know about a topic, thereby enhancing readiness for reading. Of equal importance, learners can write about a topic, read about it, and then return to their original statement in order to apply what they just learned and to revise the original. Documenting intellectual growth this way seems to improve learning.

A Brief Retrospective

This chapter is deliberately located near the end of the book. The reason for placing this chapter after the ones on asking and answering questions, forecasting passages, understanding vocabulary, and graphically representing information is to point out that many of the teaching strategies already presented could involve writing. Students could participate orally in ReQuest, the Directed Reading-Thinking Activity, the Anticipation Guide, and Contextual Redefinition, or they could participate through writing. This chapter describes additional ways to capitalize on the power of writing before reading.

Writing Tasks

Tasks are the assigned work students are expected to complete, and are the basic units of instruction teachers manipulate as they move through the school day. The following illustrates different types of writing tasks that might be assigned before having students read.

- Teacher A displays key words from a unit on Brazil and asks students to write an essay that includes all the words. The students then read about Brazil, check their essays for accuracy, and modify them if necessary.

- Teacher B asks students to brainstorm what should be included in a brochure they will produce promoting Brazil to potential tourists. After the brainstorming session, students read in order to determine what else their brochures should include.

- Teacher C asks students to write what they think they would like best about visiting Brazil. The students then read about Brazil.

- Teacher D gives students 5 minutes to write whatever they want about Brazil. The students then read about this country.

The assignments of teachers A through D illustrate three distinguishing features of writing tasks. These features can be classified on continuums of directed/free, personal/impersonal, and conventional/enriched. Figure 8 displays a feature matrix of the types of tasks assigned by Teachers A through D.

Figure 8
Feature Matrix of Representative Teachers' Types of Writing Tasks

Teacher	Direct	Free	Impersonal	Personal	Conventional	Enriched
A	+	-	+	-	+	-
B	+	-	+	-	-	+
C	+	-	-	+	+	-
D	-	+	+/-	+/-	+/-	+/-

Directed/Free Writing

As Figure 8 shows, Teachers A, B, and C provide directed tasks; they order a particular type of writing from their students each time a writing task is assigned. Conversely, Teacher D offers free writing tasks. This teacher expects his or her students to write about a certain topic, but the exact nature of the task is left up to the individual. Some authorities might argue that defining the topic for students makes the writing task directed, but here it is considered free if that is all the teacher does before offering individual assistance.

Personal/Impersonal Writing

The writing tasks of Teachers A, B, and C can be classified on a personal/impersonal continuum. (Teacher D cannot be classified on this continuum because his or her students decide what to write, and their choices will vary.) Teacher C assigns personal tasks; they relate what is being studied to students' lives. Teacher C asks students to describe what they would like about Brazil. Students' feelings are elicited and applied to the topic of study. Personal writing tasks connect students' own experiences, beliefs, and feelings with the topic being studied. On the other hand, Teachers A and B assign impersonal tasks. These assignments do not connect the subject matter directly with students' lives. Although impersonal tasks might have students call up what they know about a topic, these tasks ignore the actual experiences and reactions individuals have relative to the topic.

Conventional/Enriched Writing

Finally, Teachers A and B assign tasks that differ on the conventional/enriched continuum. (Teacher D cannot be classified on this continuum either because some students might choose conventional writing and some might choose enriched writing.) Teacher A presents conventional tasks. Teacher A has students write traditional papers that are found mainly in school settings. The conventional tasks of Teacher A emphasize academic concerns and bear little relation to the writing done outside of school. In contrast, Teacher B provides students with tasks that are enriched and have practical significance. Teacher B always designates a relevant writing form (e.g, a brochure) and an audience (e.g., potential tourists to Brazil).

A Final Word About Writing Tasks

Given the possible types of writing tasks presented by Teachers A, B, C, and D, which are best? On which end of the continuums should writing before reading tasks lie? Should they be directed or free, enriched or conventional, personal or impersonal?

A balanced program of writing before reading tasks seems most desirable. Directed writing contributes to learning, but students also should engage in free writing to enhance their learning from text. In addition, conventional and enriched tasks have merits relative to each. Summarizing a passage seems to be as important as retelling a passage in a letter to a friend. Personal and impersonal writing also deserve attention. Connecting personal experiences and values to a topic seems as important as maintaining an objective impersonal stance about a topic.

Writing Lessons

Designing tasks is only part of the strategy of using writing to enhance reading. Tasks define what the finished product is to be, but they do not specify the process students are to follow. In other words, telling students to produce a brochure about Brazil differs from teaching students how to produce such a brochure. Teaching students how to complete tasks is another dimension of instruction. This section emphasizes five writing strategies and describes how teachers and students can work together to complete certain tasks.

Identification With a Story Character

Marino, Gould, and Haas (1985) reported the benefits of having students identify with a story character through writing before reading about the character. The students' writing before reading task was directed, enriched, and personal. The lesson-based task follows:

> Pretend you are a young person in 1845. You are a pioneer heading for the Oregon country. You and your family have stopped to make camp for the night on the Snake River when you meet a group of young orphans. The oldest is a 13-year-old boy who tells you of his determination to carry on with his father's plans to take the family to Oregon. John, you learn, is a very brave and clever boy who has just saved his sister from drowning. Write a letter home to your grandparents describing this boy and the story he has told you. (p. 204)

Note that this task was directed (teacher prescribed what was to be written), contained a relevant form (letter), an audience (grandparents), and was personal (pretend to be a young person).

The experimental group consisted of 30 fourth-grade students. They were given 30 minutes to write, and, immediately after writing, they were given 30 minutes to read the 2,000 word passage about Oregon from which the writing task was derived. Before reading the passage about Oregon, the 30 control group students wrote about an interesting event that actually happened to them. A written recall test of the Oregon story was given the next day.

The experimental subjects recalled more about the passage than the control subjects, and low achieving readers seemed to perform especially well with the treatment. As the researchers explained, their results seemed to occur partly as a function of the personal nature of the task. Students responded affectively to the character, John; many students wrote about sharing fictitious events and a close friendship with him. Emotionally identifying with the character in the story before reading seemed to promote comprehension. In addition, the researchers attributed part of the benefit of their task to the audience that was specified. Writing to an audience such as grandparents (even if they are pretend) seemed to enhance the task.

To summarize, Identification With a Story Character, as presented by Marino, Gould, and Haas (1985), consists of three steps.

1. Design a task that elicits identification with a story character.

2. Have students write in response to the task.

3. Have students read the passage from which the task was derived.

Guided Writing Procedure

The Guided Writing Procedure (GWP) (Smith & Bean, 1980) was designed in part to help students synthesize and retain content area material. The lesson-based, 2-day procedure that follows is a slight adaptation of the original GWP description.

Day One

1. Have students brainstorm what they know about an upcoming topic of study (volcanoes) and record their responses on a chalkboard or overhead transparency. A possible list follows:

   Volcanoes
   lava
   destruction
   ashes
   hot
   steam
   Mt. St. Helens
   eruption
   crater
   dangerous
   fiery

2. Identify categories that encompass the brainstormed terms (physical qualities, descriptions, examples) and list details that support the category titles.

3. Represent the category titles and their details in forms such as an Outline, Web, or Graphic Organizer.

   I. Physical Qualities
      A. Crater
      B. Eruption
         1. lava
         2. ashes
         3. steam

   II. Description
      A. Fiery
         1. hot
      B. Dangerous
         1. destruction

   III. Example
      A. Mt. St. Helens

4. Have students write about the topic, using the graphically presented information.

5. Have students read a passage related to the topic of study to determine how their papers could be expanded or modified. For example, students might search for additional information about the physical qualities of volcanoes.

As can be seen, the first three GWP steps in Day One merge List-Group-Label with the procedures for graphically representing information presented earlier in this book. The steps in the Day One GWP neatly connect these strategies before writing and reading.

Day Two

1. Display a few students' papers using an overhead projector. Examples of good and poor writing should be demonstrated, and the samples might be selected from students not currently in class in order to avoid potential embarrassment. Revise the papers according to content as well as two or three of the writing criteria shown in Figure 9.

Figure 9
Possible Writing Criteria

	High			Low
• Passage Organization				
Informational Writing Major and minor points are distinguishable; topic sentence(s) stated and supported with relevant details.	4	3	2	1
Narrative Stories Story plot has identifiable beginning, middle, and end with characters introduced, a problem, and a believable or logical solution.	4	3	2	1
• Engagement The paper grasps the reader's attention by presenting vivid language in imaginative, effective ways; words are included that define ideas sharply and clearly.	4	3	2	1
• Sentence Structure Sentences are well-formed complete thoughts with no run-ons.	4	3	2	1
• Spelling All familiar words are spelled correctly; any misspellings of unfamiliar words are quite close to the correct form.	4	3	2	1

2. Have students revise their papers according to the content and writing criteria demonstrated in Figure 9. Teachers frequently have students evaluate a partner's composition before having them rewrite.

The GWP has some research support for its effectiveness in enhancing learning from text (Konopak, Martin, & Martin, 1987; Martin & Konopak, 1987; Martin, Konopak, & Martin, 1986). For example, Martin, Konopak, and Martin reported that high school juniors reading a 500-word passage on the California Gold Rush benefited from the GWP when compared with control group students who read the passage and completed word identification and short answer comprehension tasks.

In particular, the GWP students produced higher order concepts more frequently than the control group, and they synthesized information from their brainstorming session and from their reading.

It is important to realize that the results obtained by the studies reported here will not necessarily occur with other students reading other passages in other situations. The circumstances present during the studies by Marino, Gould, and Haas (1985) and Martin, Konopak, and Martin (1986) probably will not be present when other educators try the teaching strategies. Perhaps the greatest value of this research is its clear illustration of specific ways that writing before reading benefited particular students' learning from text. Educators can use these studies to suggest—not guarantee—ways that writing might influence learning.

Hennings Sequence

Hennings (1982) described a sequence of steps designed to clarify the organization of informational content. The Hennings Sequence is a unit- or lesson-based strategy originally intended for elementary school children, although it can be adapted for all grade levels. Used as a unit-based activity, students will be able to focus on the central question posed to them for the unit. It synthesizes much of the current thinking about helping students organize factual information. Hennings presented her sequence as a way to prepare students for reading informational text, although many of the eight steps will be familiar to those who have guided students through research reports.

1. *Factstorming.* Students first become familiar with a topic through viewing films and slides, interviewing people, going on excursions, reading, talking, and doing and observing. Students then brainstorm what they know about the topic, calling out information for someone to record on a chalkboard.

2. *Categorizing facts.* Students next organize the terms randomly produced during the first step. The categories can be determined and recorded several ways. One way is to circle a word with a colored marker and circle related words with the same color. Another way is to produce a Data Chart. Data Charts consist of a grid with headings always over the columns and occasionally beside the rows. The students or the teacher may provide the headings, and the headings may be given before or after factstorming. Data Chart cells are filled by students on their own or by teachers with student input. Factstormed information should be in-

cluded, and students might consult reading materials, adults, and other sources of information in order to fill the cells with facts. Intermediate students might employ the Data Chart for tigers displayed in Figure 10. A high school natural science class might use the Data Chart for flowering plants shown in Figure 11.

3. *Drafting cohesive paragraphs.* Once information is categorized, students draft paragraphs. Hennings recommends that students share the work by having groups take responsibility for certain categories of information. If a data chart is used, then students can be directed to translate into a paragraph the information contained in a column, row, or cell.

Figure 10
Data Chart for Tigers

Where do tigers live?

What do tigers eat?

What dangers do tigers face?

Figure 11
Data Chart for Flowering Plants

	Herbaceous Dicot	Woody Dicot	Herbaceous Monocot	Woody Monocot
Common				
Types				
Internal				
Stem				
Structure				
External				
Stem				
Structure				

4. *Sequencing paragraphs into a logical whole.* Students share their paragraphs and decide on the best order for the final report. A Data Chart would be helpful in framing the order of paragraphs.

5. *Drafting introductions and conclusions.* The introduction and conclusion of a paper seem to come more readily after, rather than before, the contents of a report are written. To write an introduction and a conclusion, students need to know what they are introducing and concluding. Hennings suggested composing the beginning and ending of a paper as a teacher-guided, group writing activity.

6. *Organizing the parts into a cohesive report.* A few students put together a final draft of the paper. A main title and subheadings for each of the categories should be included.

7. *Interpreting similar pieces of discourse.* Students who have gone through the first six steps of the Hennings Sequence probably understand the structure of informational content better than students who only have read such material. Writers seem to have an advantage over those who only read because writers realize how passages are put together. Taking what students have learned about the structure of materials, teachers guide students to find the same structures in what they read. For instance, students can use a Data Chart to recover essential information from new passages. At this point, Data Charts become tools for postreading rather than prewriting.

8. *Summarizing, synthesizing, and judging.* The final step calls for students to return to writing, only this time the writing is based directly on information obtained through reading. In the case of the Data Chart in Figure 11, students might be asked to read a new passage about plants and summarize the internal and external structure of woody dicots, explain the differences between herbaceous monocots and herbaceous dicots, or judge which plant is most helpful to humans. These new tasks illustrate the give and take between comprehending and composing.

The Hennings Sequence collapses some steps of the writing before reading process that the GWP separates, but Hennings also separates some steps that the GWP collapses. For instance, the GWP step 4 (have students write about the topic) is separated into steps 3, 4, 5, and 6 by Hennings. When taken together, these strategies offer a complete view of a writing before reading procedure.

Free Writing

Free Writing gained popularity in the 1970s (Elbow, 1973) as a way to release students who had difficulty getting the writing act started. Today educators (for example, Holmes & Moulton, 1997; Ollman, 1996) still tout Free Writing as a way to loosen writers and get their ideas flowing in either a lesson-based or unit-based format.

The important thing in Free Writing is to continually produce words. Students should not worry about written mechanics or structure as they write thoughts in whatever order they come. The standard recommendation for students who complain "I don't know what to write" is to have them copy "I don't know what to write" until some thoughts occur. One way to stimulate Free Writing is to play music and have students write whatever occurs to them while listening. This strategy is a non-threatening way to help students record their thoughts fluently.

Free Writing can be used for preparing students to learn from text. It is the strategy Teacher D used ("for the next 5 minutes, write whatever you want about Brazil"). Although Free Writing typically calls for students to originate their own topics, one variation is to assign a topic and have students write freely about it for a certain period of time. Free Writing is similar to brainstorming because students recall and record information according to whatever associations occur to them. This strategy can be motivating and informative for students who are preparing to study.

Having students maintain content journals is a good way to foster Free Writing. Content journals, also called dialogue journals or learning logs, are appropriate for all school subjects. Students record in a notebook their insights about the topics being studied in class. Content journals are as a cross between diaries and class notes. They are like diaries because they contain personal thoughts and like class notes because they focus on subject matter information.

Having students write freely in their journals before reading can be accomplished several ways. Many teachers provide 5 to 10 minutes of class time each day for students to record their journal entries. When a prereading strategy is appropriate, teachers might have students write in their journals at the beginning of the class. Teachers might list key words from an upcoming chapter and have students write freely about them as prereading preparation. Questions might be asked such as, How well can I explain these concepts? How much can I say about them? What do I know or not know about this topic? Students can share what they write if they wish. Students date each entry and maintain a table of contents. In this way students will have a record of their learning as they try to deal with the central question posed for the unit.

Quick Writes

Quick Writes (Moore, Moore, Cunningham, & Cunningham, 1998; also called Write Now by Rillero, Zambo, Cleland, & Ryan, 1996) is an easily implemented, lesson-based strategy that can prepare students for new material to be learned or enable them to review previously learned material in preparation for new content. Quick Writes begins by posing a question such as (a) or (b) to students and having them react to it in writing.

(a) Today we begin a new unit on the weather. In the next 30 seconds write down all the words you know that you think of when you think of the weather.

(b) Before we begin talking about water conservation, write down everything you know about the concept of conservation. You have 1 minute.

The intent of these questions is to preview the topic and get students to access their prior knowledge and thinking about a topic. Additionally, it gives teachers a notion of what students know about the topic. Once students have listed what they know, you may want to have them tell what they have written down as you list their associations on the board or overhead. Point out to students that this is the starting point of the lesson, which is akin to the beginning of List-Group-Label described in Chapter 4 or K-W-L described in Chapter 5.

Quick Writes also can serve as a means to get students to synthesize what they learned from a previous lesson. In this case questions such as (c) and (d) might be considered.

(c) We have been learning about climates. In 45 seconds list as many different climates as you can.

(d) Yesterday's history lesson had some difficult ideas to be learned. Write down at least one idea that you think you don't understand well enough.

Once this activity is completed and students have shared what they know, you will know if any reteaching may be necessary before moving on to new material. Additionally, this helps students self-assess their own learning and monitor how well they have understood the material.

Quick Writes is motivating and enables students to improve their level of understanding. The strategy can be adapted easily to whatever is being studied and to the ability level of the students.

Direct Instruction With Writing Before Reading

The goal of having students write independently before they read can be met through the cycle of instructional events. To illustrate, one of the basic components of the GWP and the Hennings Sequence, brainstorming information, can be faded from a teacher-directed to a student-directed process.

Demonstration

Begin the demonstration stage by labeling the strategy. Tell students that writing before reading is one way to improve learning, and brainstorming is an important part of this. Briefly define brainstorming and explain its relevance. Depending on the age and maturity of the students, specify actual instances in the present and future when brainstorming would be appropriate as a part of writing before reading.

The next step is to model the strategy, which frequently can be done in a few minutes. For instance, if you want your students to brainstorm what they know about a topic, you might say, "Give me a topic, and watch how I brainstorm what I know about it." After brainstorming for awhile, stop and explain what you just did. Articulate how to use the strategy: "Did you notice how I wrote very quickly as I called out what I knew? And did you see how quickly I worked? You should think and write quickly when you brainstorm."

Guided Practice

After demonstrating what you want your students to do, give them a chance to do it. The first time they try the strategy might be as a large group: "Now it's your turn, class. Here's the topic, so call out everything you know about it just as I did." Several students might record words the class calls out. Provide feedback about their performance: "Good, you're moving quickly. Keep the words coming; we'll work with them later."

Teachers frequently have students work in pairs or small groups during the guided practice stage. Working together, students share insights about the process and jointly solve problems. Guided practice with feedback should continue until students seem adept with the strategy.

Independent Application

In order to foster independent application, have students use the strategy once they are skillful with it: "This passage contains vital information. If you understand its key points, you'll understand the fundamental concepts we'll be covering the next 4 weeks. Therefore, take some time and write what you know about this topic before reading." Assistance then can be provided as needed.

It is important to realize that independent application is meant to prompt students to do what they have been taught previously. Simply telling students to write before they read without demonstrating the strategy and providing guided practice defies the tenets of direct, explicit instruction.

Summary

The rationale of writing before reading as an aid to learning is similar to the rationale of the other prereading strategies presented in this book. The fact that writing provides a permanent record of thoughts is an additional benefit. Writing tasks can be classified on continuums of directed/free, personal/impersonal, and conventional/enriched. A balanced program of writing tasks seems most appropriate for enhancing learning from text. Five strategies for helping students complete writing before reading tasks and promote learning are Identification With a Story Character, the Guided Writing Procedure, the Hennings Sequence, Free Writing, and Quick Writes. The brainstorming component of these strategies can be taught readily through a program of direct instruction.

Chapter 7

Combining Prereading Activities

PURPOSE

This chapter shows how to combine prereading activities with one another and with regular classroom instruction. Examples come from English/language arts, social studies, science, and interdisciplinary units of instruction. They are concrete illustrations of prereading planning and teaching that teachers have reported in professional literature.

Examples

1. A middle grade *novel unit* based on *Shabanu, Daughter of the Wind* by Suzanne F. Staples provides multiple entry points.

2. *Shakespearean drama* typically challenges secondary school readers. Prereading preparation helps readers meet the challenges.

3. A *human population investigation* focusing on one's local community requires support prior to reading.

4. An *environmental thematic unit* can link students' study of the science, social studies, mathematics, and language arts of preservation and conservation. Preparing students for such integrated study is crucial.

5. *Community links* directly involve students' family members and school neighbors in support of reading and learning.

6. *Literature-based history units* rely on book authors to prepare students for learning.

7. *Issues-centered geography* centers around long-standing social concerns. Getting students ready to examine the issues promotes learning.

Seven units of instruction are summarized here. In the first part of this chapter, we emphasize each unit's introductory activities. We show how units creatively combine prereading activities according to classroom situations. The second part of this chapter provides brief concluding comments on similarities among the examples.

Novel Unit

Shabanu, Daughter of the Wind is a 240-page novel that tends to hold the interest of middle school language arts students. It focuses on a 12-year-old nomadic Islamic girl in Pakistan. Numerous activities appropriately guide students through the text (see Benedicty, 1995).

A good beginning is to enrich students' understandings of the setting: desert life in Pakistan. Display photographs and slides of rural Middle Eastern life and show videos. Elicit students' images and information they have of this topic. Someone from the class or community might share first-hand experiences with this region of the world. List housing, transportation, and clothing features mentioned in the book and portray them as vividly as possible. Students might benefit from imagining themselves living in tents, riding camels, and wearing turbans. Burning incense and playing Middle Eastern music might help students to visualize this setting.

Introducing unfamiliar words that are crucial to understanding the novel but that are not fully explained is a good way to balance vocabulary and passage understandings. To illustrate, desert oases play a large role in *Shabanu*. As part of the introduction to the novel, display *oasis* before the class, call attention to its pronunciation, and then develop in-depth knowledge of its meaning. Ask students to recall what they already know about oases, present pictures of them, and create analogies between oases and locations in the local vicinity. Connect this individual term to the overall novel by explaining how it is a central part of the setting.

After viewing scenes from a Middle Eastern desert, students might begin to wonder what life there would be like. Pique their interest by asking what differences they would expect if they moved to rural living in Pakistan. By focusing on one feature—transportation, for instance—have students imagine all the ways life with camels would differ from life with automobiles.

Prereading preparation also can be accomplished by focusing attention on a central question such as one of the following:

- What is the same and what is different about my life and Shabanu's life?
- How does Shabanu change during the course of the novel?
- How do the characters' attitudes toward obedience affect their actions in this novel?

Reading aloud the first few chapters is a good way to support students' initial efforts with the novel. Demonstrate interest in *Shabanu* by commenting what you find fascinating and what you hope to learn in the future. Produce a schedule so everyone knows when certain chapters, the whole book, and culminating activities such as an in-class essay exam are to be completed.

Shakespearean Drama Unit

Macbeth, Hamlet, Romeo and Juliet, The Tempest, and *The Merchant of Venice* are a few of William Shakespeare's plays that continue to challenge secondary school readers. Prereading preparation goes far in helping students meet these challenges (Adams, 1995; Breen, 1993; Rothenberg & Watts, 1997).

K-W-L is a good beginning activity. Students who express what they know and what they want to know generate readiness to learn. With *Macbeth* students collectively might decide that they want to learn why Shakespeare is believed to be a great writer and the characteristics of literary tragedy.

To help students access the contents of *Macbeth*, highlight tragedy as a central theme. Help students call up what they already know about how heroes cope with the idea of either fate or free will underlying events. Using prior course contents and personal experiences, help students develop working understandings of fate, free will, tragedy, and hero. Relate political leaders such as Richard Nixon and Bill Clinton and popular figures such as the *Star Wars* characters Darth Vader and Luke Skywalker to these conceptions.

Develop understandings of the play's setting: Scotland in the year 1050. Post a map of Scotland and note the country's geography. Decorate the classroom with visual and concrete representations of the setting's clothing, architecture, religion, warfare, and politics. Discuss what students already know about these aspects of medieval life.

Another key to understanding *Macbeth* involves its structure. Remind students how playwrights develop characters, plot, and theme and encourage attention to these features. Also note differences between silently reading a play, orally reading it, and performing it. When reading silently or orally, encourage students to visualize actions, costumes, and sets. Additionally, have students predict Macbeth's actions, speculate on Shakespeare's future use of witches in the story, and be ready for well-known phrases such as *fair is foul and foul is fair* along with unfamiliar terms such as *thane.*

Along with providing a foundation for the entirety of *Macbeth*, prepare students for particular sections within the play. For instance, at the beginning of Act I, you might prepare students as follows: "We know that Macbeth is a heroic figure. Pay close attention to lines reflecting this. What is the atmosphere or feeling established in the beginning of the play? Watch to see if it changes" (Rothenberg & Watts, 1997, p. 537). At the beginning of Act V, you might advise students to watch for Macbeth's return to his former dignity. Experiencing the text as a script is far more powerful than reading it like a novel; therefore, prepare for, rehearse, and perform selected sections of *Macbeth* with as much theatrical accompaniment as possible.

Human Population Investigation Unit

Population growth affects the world's natural resources and humanity's quality of life. Secondary students can examine these effects by investigating population density in their own community (Wilder, 1998).

Introduce the human population investigation with Cat Stevens's song, "Where Do the Children Play?" Talk with the class about relationships among the song's concerns and population growth. Then explain population density (number of people/unit of area) and have students calculate it for the classroom. Extend the concept of population density to the school then to the local community (*community* is flexible; it can be defined as a county, town, or portion of a large metropolis). Next, pose a central question such as: How has the population density of our human community affected the natural community?

After launching the unit, form groups of four students each who select the role of either historian, mathematician, naturalist, or civil engineer. For each role provide task cards that direct students to particular aspects of the research. For instance, historians might address a question such as: How has the percentage of local land devoted for particular uses changed over time? Civil engineers might address the question: What natural resources do the community's public services utilize? Consult public service agencies such as chambers of commerce, planning and zoning commissions, and census bureaus for print materials and local officials.

To guide students' research efforts and data collection, present a chart such as the one the follows with dates as row headings and subtopics such as population density and water supply as column headings.

	Population Density	Water Supply	Waste Disposal	Recreation Facilities
Present				
1975				
1950				
1925				

Groups share their findings as they complete their research, discussing similarities and discrepancies. Returning to the original central question, talk about how population density has affected the natural community. Culminate the unit with the groups producing and displaying public service announcements for the local community.

Environmental Thematic Unit

Thematic units center disciplinary study around common concepts. For instance, middle grade reading/language arts, social studies, science, and mathematics can be integrated when studying environmental concepts of conservation and preservation (Heller, 1997).

Begin the 2-week thematic unit for sixth grade with an open-ended question: What concerns you the most about our environment? This question taps adolescents' feelings and understandings while framing their thoughts about a relevant topic. A video on the environment is appropriate for clarifying significant issues. Other introductory activities include a discovery walk in which students tour a nearby area and then record all they observed, a microenvironment activity in which students draw in minute detail what they see in a confined space (for example, five square inches of lawn or a piece of tree bark), or a scavenger hunt for items such as something that was under a rock and something the student is glad is in this environment (see the America Online Teacher Information Network [www.minnetonka.k12.mn.us/support/science/tools/earthmonth.html] and the Columbia Education Center [www.col-ed.org/cur/sci/sci79.txt]).

After introducing unit contents, present the unit objectives, materials, activities, and assignments in the form of a self-assessment checklist containing items such the following:

____ made a recyclable materials cover for my Environmental Awareness portfolio.

____ read at least one book about environmental issues and responded in my journal.

____ shared my writing-in-progress with a friend.

____ I made suggestions for our list of environmental research questions and tried to find the answer to one or more questions. (Heller, 1997, p. 335)

A home survey is a good ongoing assignment for this unit. Involving family members and having volunteers report their findings each day helps unify the lessons and promote research. For instance, one student's comment about washing the family car led students to wonder about the advantages of washing cars at home or at a commercial site.

The open-ended question, video, outside observation, checklist, and survey prepare students for what they read and write. Additional preparation directly linked with literacy consists of teacher read alouds of environmental picture books, book chapters, and poems. Students can respond in journals to the read alouds, and pattern their own environmental writings according to models such as the following:

A Goat Wandered into the Junkyard (Jack Prelutsky, 1990)

Just a Dream (Chris Van Allsburg, 1990)

Keepers of the Earth (Michael Caduto and Joseph Bruchac, 1989)

Sarah Cynthia Sylvia Stout (Shel Silverstein, 1974)

The Great Kapok Tree (Lynne Cherry, 1990)

Have students read and respond to a self-selected book that addresses an environmental issue. The books might come from personal, classroom, school, and town libraries. Responses to self-selected books are recorded in journals along with reactions to read-alouds, videos, and discussions.

One unit culmination is a class newsletter. The newsletter, *Recycler's Digest*, could contain news reports, fiction, and poetry that students produce during the unit. The final class event might include a guided tour of a recycling center, a trash pickup, or a tree planting.

Community Links Unit

Cognitive practices such as previewing passages and questioning oneself about upcoming ideas are crucial aspects of reading, but they are only part of the picture. The social and cultural settings that embed adolescents' reading and learning also deserves attention. Making use of the community links available to students—especially to those students who commonly risk academic failure—can be productive. A junior high school unit integrating literacy and Mexican American culture demonstrates such links (Brozo, Valerio, & Salazar, 1996).

Begin the unit with a party, where information can be shared among parents, teachers, administrators, and students. This opening event outlines unit purposes and activities, signals its importance, and enlists family support.

Packets of reading and writing activities for students to complete with family members explicitly connect home and school. Involve students and parents in an activity in which they read aloud to each other stories by Hispanic authors that address authentic Hispanic cultural experiences. Another activity might call for parents and students to brew manzanilla, a native tea described in a short story.

Community resources can be tapped several ways. Take students on a tour of a neighbor's herb garden, visit a local university during a Cinco de Mayo celebration, and participate in a guest presentation by a local Mexican American scholar.

The core text of the unit could be Rudolfo Anaya's culturally relevant novel, *Bless Me, Ultima* (1972). Additional readings could include short stories and informational passages by Hispanic authors such as Sandra Cisneros and Gary Soto. Most students will identify with the characters and conflicts of these passages. Assign students to cooperative literature discussion groups consisting of four individuals, and instruct them to fulfill roles such as discussion director and vocabulary enricher that have been modeled extensively. The students can read assigned portions of the text prior to the group meetings, then complete forms with information befitting their roles during the meetings. After each chapter of *Bless Me, Ultima*, have students write in response to previously demonstrated prompts such as the following:

- Compose three questions you would like to have answered in the next chapter.
- Did this reading remind you of something that has happened in your life? Describe the incident.

- Do the values, ideas, thoughts, or actions in this story confirm or conflict with your own personal values? How? (Brozo, Valerio, & Salazar, 1996, p. 168)

Literature-Based History Unit

Middle grade World War II (WWII) instructional units grounded in literature offer compelling perspectives to this complex subject (Ruddiman, 1997). Historical literature makes the subject intriguing and shows that history is about people as well as events.

Literature-based units require books that are written at different levels of difficulty, that present trustworthy ideas, and that engage readers. Sets of the following titles are appropriate for a sixth-grade WWII unit (Kornfeld, 1994):

The Devil's Arithmetic (Jane Yolen, 1988)

Journey to Topaz (Yoshiko Uchida, 1971)

The Machine Gunners (Robert Westfall, 1976)

Maus I (Art Spiegelman, 1986)

The Road to Memphis (Mildred Taylor, 1990)

To begin this unit, explain how historical literature compellingly presents aspects of an event like WWII and how historical fiction blends elements of fact with pretense. Then form literature study groups around books, assign minimum numbers of pages to read each day, and ensure that individuals know how to respond to what they read during group time.

The essential prereading preparation performed during this unit is providing students opportunities to interact with well-written and appropriately selected books. Initial readings can lead to additional readings with minimal teacher intervention. For instance, the initial sentences and story opening of *The Devil's Arithmetic* prepare students for the remaining chapters. Picture books such as *Faithful Elephants* (Yukio Tsuchiya, 1988) and *Rose Blanche* (Roberto Innocenti, 1985) that address mature WWII subject matter in a very accessible manner encourage additional reading. Teacher read alouds of short sections of *Along the Tracks* (Tamar Bergman, 1991) and *The Little Fishes* (Erik Haugaard, 1967) prompt students to read and learn even more about WWII. Students also can form mixed groups and read certain short passages from books such as the following:

The Crystal Nights (Michele Murray, 1973)

Diary of a Young Girl (Anne Frank, 1994)

The Endless Steppe (Esther Hautzig, 1968)

Farewell to Manzanar (Jeanne Houston, 1983)

Night (Elie Wiesel, 1989)

Number the Stars (Lois Lowry, 1989)

The Upstairs Room (Johanna Reiss, 1972)

Year of Impossible Goodbyes (Sook Nyul Choi, 1991)

Various culminating activities allow students to express their thoughts of what they read and learn about WWII. Students can write fictional diaries, perform skits, and compose newspaper articles and editorials about incidents in the books. They can produce and share biographies of Allied and Axis leaders, picture books of anti-Nazi families in prewar Germany, and models of internment camps.

Issues-Centered Geography Unit

Units centered around problems that have persisted over the years encourage students to connect their concerns, interests, and experiences with unit contents. Students who actively inquire into social studies issues such as appropriate limits to freedom of speech and reasons for war process facts and ideas mindfully.

To provide prereading preparation for issues-centered instruction in ninth-grade world geography classes, ask the central question: "Why should we care about Latin America and the Caribbean?" (Rossi & Pace, 1998, p. 389). Although this question runs the risk of defining countries according to U.S. criteria, it is meant to be provoke thinking, engage emotions, and invigorate students' inquiries into the area's economic, political, and cultural conditions.

To introduce the unit and its central question, have students complete a questionnaire that assesses attitudes toward Latin America. Then have students complete a map exercise in which they act as corporate executives planning to move their product to market. Discussion of these two launch activities foreshadows the central question and arouses interest in reading and learning about the topic.

Unit reading materials should include sources from the Internet, a computerized database of maps and national statistics, and periodical articles about Columbia, Cuba, Haiti, Mexico, and Panama. Teacher-directed and independent readings and discussions of these materials generate considerable information. To identify, gather, and organize important information, present a chart such as the one that follows with countries as row headings and column headings such as *physical geography* and *history.*

	Physical Geography	History
Columbia		
Cuba		
Haiti		
Mexico		
Panama		

As students add information to the chart, they learn to control the data they encounter and address the central question. Students then reference this information in order to participate in culminating activities such as immigration policy debates, mock presentations about trade to the U.S. Senate Foreign Relations Committee, letters to the U.S. president, and essay writing.

Concluding Comments

The units of instruction described in this chapter have much in common. One, they demonstrate the feasibility of prereading preparation. The examples show teachers using classroom time well by priming students for upcoming subject matter. Reading aloud a WWII picture book differs from explaining the structure of Shakespearean drama, yet both prepare students for future reading and learning. These descriptions show teachers efficiently setting learning in motion, enabling learners to be productive.

Second, prereading practices are flexible; they work in numerous situations. For example, most instruction described here includes a central question:

- What is the same and what is different about my life and Shabanu's life?
- Why is Shakespeare considered to be a great writer?
- How has the population density of our human community affected the natural community?
- What concerns you most about our environment?
- Why should we care about Latin America and the Caribbean?

Two units described here present Data Charts for students to complete, and two specify read alouds as introductory practices. Employing common practices such as central questions, Data Charts, and read alouds across such diverse units indicates the flexibility of these prereading practices. They are malleable, fitting countless situations.

Third, the examples presented here demonstrate how readily prereading options can be combined. One unit combines discussion of a folk song with the presentation of a Data Chart; another links a map exercise with a Data Chart. By showing instruction varying from classroom to classroom and unit to unit, the examples suggest myriad combinations for future situations.

Finally, the examples point to the need for principled decision making. As Chapter 1 explained, effective instructional planning accounts for learners' expected outcomes, motivation, content knowledge, attention, and learning strategies. The units presented here address these factors directly. Every example leads to certain learnings by arousing curiosity, tapping prior knowledge, focusing on important ideas, and enlisting learning strategies. The examples in this chapter join what has been presented in earlier chapters to guide instructional decision makers to effective prereading activities for content area reading and learning.

References

Adams, P.E. (1995). Teaching *Romeo and Juliet* in the nontracked English classroom. *Journal of Reading, 38*, 424–432.

Alexander, P.A., & Jetton, T.L. (2000). Learning from text: A multidimensional and developmental perspective. In M.L. Kamil, P.B. Mosenthal, P.D. Pearson, & R. Barr (Eds.), *Handbook of reading research: Volume III.* Mahwah, NJ: Erlbaum.

Alvermann, D.E., & Phelps, S.F. (1998). *Content reading and literacy: Succeeding in today's diverse classrooms* (2nd ed.). Boston: Allyn and Bacon.

Ash, B.H. (1992). Student-made questions: One way into a literary text. *English Journal, 82*, 61–64.

America Online Teacher Information Network. Earth care: A unit on the environment. Available online: http://www.minnetonka.k12.mn.us/support/science/tools/earthmonth.html

Aukerman, R.C. (1972). *Reading in the secondary school.* New York: McGraw-Hill.

Barron, R.F., & Earle, R.A. (1973). An approach for vocabulary instruction. In H.L. Herber & R.F. Barron (Eds.), *Research in reading in the content areas: Second year report* (pp. 84–100). Syracuse, NY: Syracuse University Reading and Language Arts Center.

Bean, T.W. (2000). Reading in the content areas: Social constructivist dimensions. In M.L. Kamil, P.B. Mosenthal, P.D. Pearson, & R. Barr (Eds.), *Handbook of reading research: Volume III.* Mahwah, NJ: Erlbaum.

Bear, D.R., & McIntosh, M.E. (1990). Directed reading-thinking activities: Four activities to promote thinking and study habits in social studies. *Social Education, 54*, 385–388.

Beck, I.L., Omanson, R.C., & McKeown, M.G. (1982). An instructional redesign of reading lessons: Effects on comprehension. *Reading Research Quarterly, 17*, 462–481.

Benedicty, A. (1995). Reading Shabanu: Creating multiple entry points for diverse readers. *Voices from the Middle, 2*, 12–17.

Branley, F.M. (Ed.). (1963). *Reader's Digest science readers.* Pleasantville, NY: Reader's Digest Services.

Bransford, J.D., & Johnson, M.K. (1972). Contextual prerequisites for understanding: Some investigations of comprehension and recall. *Journal of Verbal Learning and Verbal Behavior, 11*, 717–726.

Breen, K.T. (1993). Taking Shakespeare from the page to the stage. *English Journal, 82*, 46–48.

Brozo, W.G., & Simpson, M.L. (1999). *Readers, teachers, learners: Expanding literacy across the content areas* (3rd ed.). Upper Saddle River, NJ: Merrill.

Brozo, W.G., Valerio, P.C., & Salazar, M.M. (1996). A walk through Gracie's garden: Literacy and cultural explorations in a Mexican American junior high school. *Journal of Adolescent & Adult Literacy, 40*, 164–170.

Carr, E., & Ogle, D. (1987). K-W-L Plus: A strategy for comprehension and summarization. *Journal of Reading, 30*, 626–631.

Chen, H.S., & Graves, M.F. (1998). Previewing challenging reading selections for ESL students. *Journal of Adolescent & Adult Literacy, 41*, 570–571.

Columbia Education Center. Integrated unit on Nevada solid waste disposal. Available online: http://www.col-ed.org/cur/sci/sci79.txt

De Garmo, C. (1896). *Herbart and the Herbartians*. New York: Charles Scribner's Sons.

Draper, W., & Bailey, A. (1978). *Steps in clothing skills* (Rev. ed.). Peoria, IL: Charles A. Bennet.

Dyson, A.H., & Freedman, S.W. (1991). Writing. In J. Flood, J.M. Jensen, D. Lapp, & J.R. Squire (Eds.), *Handbook of research on teaching the English language arts* (pp. 754–774). New York: Macmillan.

Elbow, P. (1973). *Writing without teachers*. New York: Oxford University Press.

Erickson, H.L. (1998). *Concept-based curriculum and instruction: Teaching beyond the facts*. Thousand Oaks, CA: Corwin,.

Gee, T.C., & Rakow, S.J. (1991). Content reading education: What methods do teachers prefer? *NASSP Bulletin, 75*, 104–111.

Glynn, S. (1996). Teaching with analogies: Building on the science textbook. *The Reading Teacher, 49*, 490–492.

Glynn, S.M., & DiVesta, F.J. (1977). Outline and hierarchical organization as aids for study and retrieval. *Journal of Educational Psychology, 69*, 89–95.

Graves, M.F., Cooke, C.L., & LaBerge, M.J. (1983). Effects of previewing difficult short stories on low ability junior high school students' comprehension, recall, and attitudes. *Reading Research Quarterly, 18*, 262–276.

Graves, M.F., & Graves, B.B. (1994). *Scaffolding reading experiences: Designs for student success*. Norwood, MA: Christopher-Gordon.

Guthrie, J.T., & Wigfield, A. (2000). Engagement and motivation in reading. In M.L. Kamil, P.B. Mosenthal, P.D. Pearson, & R. Barr (Eds.), *Handbook of reading research: Volume III*. Mahwah, NJ: Erlbaum.

Hayes, D.A., & Tierney, R.J. (1982). Developing reader's knowledge though analogy. *Reading Research Quarterly, 17*, 256–280.

Head, M.H., & Readence, J.E. (1992). Anticipation guides: Using prediction to promote learning from text. In E.K. Dishner, T.W. Bean, J.E. Readence, & D.W. Moore (Eds.), *Reading in the content areas: Improving classroom instruction* (3rd ed., pp. 227–233). Dubuque, IA: Kendell/Hunt.

Helfeldt, J.P., & Henk, W.A. (1990). Reciprocal question-answer relationships: An instructional technique for at-risk readers. *Journal of Reading, 33*, 509–514.

Heller, M. (1997). Reading and writing about the environment: Visions of the year 2000. *Journal of Adolescent & Adult Literacy, 40*, 332–341.

Hennings, D.G. (1982). A writing approach to reading comprehension: Schema theory in action. *Language Arts, 59*, 8–17.

Hoffman, J.V. (1992). Critical reading/thinking across the curriculum: Using I-Charts to support learning. *Language Arts, 69*, 121–127.

Holmes, V.L., & Moulton, M.R. (1997). Dialogue journals as an ESL learning strategy. *Journal of Adolescent & Adult Literacy, 40*, 616–621.

Huffman, L.E. (1996). What's in it for you? A student-directed text preview. *Journal of Adolescent & Adult Literacy, 40*, 56–57.

Huffman, L.E. (1998). Spotlighting specifics by combining focus questions with K-W-L. *Journal of Adolescent & Adult Literacy, 41*, 470–472.

Johnson, D.D., & Pearson, P.D. (1984). *Teaching reading vocabulary* (2nd ed.). New York: Holt, Rinehart & Winston.

Konopak, B.C., Martin, S.H., & Martin, M.A. (1987). An integrated communications arts approach for enhancing students' learning in content areas. *Reading Research and Instruction, 26*, 275–289.

Kornfeld, J. (1994). Using fiction to teach history: Multicultural and global perspectives of World War II. *Social Education, 58*, 281–286.

Kucan, L., & Beck, I.L. (1997). Thinking and reading comprehension research: Inquiry, instruction, and social interaction. *Review of Educational Research, 67*, 271–299.

Langer, J.A. (1981). From theory to practice: A prereading plan. *Journal of Reading, 25*, 159–156.

Laycock, S.R., & Russell, D.H. (1941). An analysis of thirty-eight how-to study manuals. *School Review, 49*, 370–379.

Lunstrum, J.P. (1981). Building motivation through the use of controversy. *Journal of Reading, 24*, 687–691.

Magorian, M. (1981). *Good night, Mr. Tom.* New York: Harper & Row.

Manzo, A.V. (1969). The ReQuest procedure. *Journal of Reading, 13*, 123–126.

Marino, J.L., Gould, S.M., & Haas, L.W. (1985). The effects of writing as a prereading activity on delayed recall of narrative text. *The Elementary School Journal, 86*, 199–205.

Martin, M.A., & Konopak, B.C. (1987). An instructional investigation of students' ideas generated during content area writing. In J.E. Readence & R.S. Baldwin (Eds.), *Research in literacy: Merging perspectives* (Thirty-sixth Yearbook of the National Reading Conference, pp. 265–271). Rochester, NY: National Reading Conference.

Martin, M.A., Konopak, B.C., & Martin, S.H. (1986). Use of the guided writing procedure to facilitate comprehension of high school text materials. In J.A. Niles & R.V. Lalik (Eds.), *Solving problems in literacy: Learners, teachers, and researchers* (Thirty-fifth Yearbook of the National Reading Conference, pp. 66–72). Rochester, NY: National Reading Conference.

Maurer, D.W. (1964). *Whiz mob.* Schenectady, NY: New College and University Press.

McConnell, S. (1992/1993). Talking drawings: A strategy for assisting learners. *Journal of Reading, 36*, 260–269.

McGinley, W.J., & Denner, P.R. (1987). Story impressions: A pre-reading/writing activity. *Journal of Reading, 31*, 248–253.

McMurry, F.M. (1909). *How to study and teaching how to study.* Boston: Houghton Mifflin.

Moore, D.W., & Moore, S.A. (1992). Possible sentences: An update. In E.K. Dishner, T.W. Bean, J.E. Readence, & D.W. Moore (Eds.), *Reading in the content areas: Improving classroom instruction* (3rd ed., pp. 303–310). Dubuque, IA: Kendall/Hunt.

Moore, D.W., Moore, S.A., Cunningham, P.M., & Cunningham, J.W. (1998). *Developing readers and writers in the content areas, K–12* (3rd ed.). New York: Longman.

Moore, D.W., & Readence, J.E. (1984). A quantitative and qualitative review of graphic organizer research. *Journal of Educational Research, 78*, 11–17.

Ogle, D. (1986). K-W-L: A teaching model that develops active reading of expository text. *The Reading Teacher, 39*, 564–570.

Ollman, H.E. (1996). Creating higher level thinking with reading response. *Journal of Adolescent & Adult Literacy, 39*, 576–581.

Palincsar, A.S., & Brown, A.L. (1984). Reciprocal teaching of comprehension fostering and monitoring activities. *Cognition and Instruction, 1*, 117–175.

Pearson, P.D., & Johnson, D.D. (1978). *Teaching reading comprehension.* New York: Holt, Rinehart & Winston.

Pittelman, S.D., Heimlich, J.E., Berglund, R.L., & French, M.P. (1991). *Semantic feature analysis: Classroom applications.* Newark, DE: International Reading Association.

Randall, S.N. (1996). Information charts: A strategy for organizing student research. *Journal of Adolescent & Adult Literacy, 39*, 536–542.

Raphael, T.E. (1984). Teaching learners about sources of information for answering comprehension questions. *Journal of Reading, 27*, 303–311.

Raphael, T.E. (1986). Teaching question answer relationships, revisited. *The Reading Teacher, 39*, 516–522.

Readence, J.E., Bean, T.W., & Baldwin, R.S. (1998). *Content area literacy: An integrated approach* (6th ed.). Dubuque, IA: Kendall/Hunt.

Rillero, P., Zambo, R., Cleland, J., & Ryan, J. (1996). Write from the start: Writing to learn science. *Science Scope, 19*, 30–32.

Rosenshine, B., & Stevens, R. (1986). Teaching functions. In M.C. Wittrock (Ed.), *Handbook of research on teaching* (3rd ed., pp. 376–391). New York: Macmillan.

Rossi, J.A., & Pace, C.M. (1998). Issues-centered instruction with low achieving high school students: The dilemmas of two teachers. *Theory and Research in Social Education, 26*, 380–409.

Rothenberg, S.S., & Watts, S.M. (1997). Students with learning difficulties meet Shakespeare: Using a scaffolded reading experience. *Journal of Adolescent & Adult Literacy, 40*, 532–539.

Ruddell, M.R. (1994). Vocabulary knowledge and comprehension: A comprehension-process view of complex literacy relationships. In R.B. Ruddell, M.R. Ruddell, & H. Singer (Eds.), *Theoretical models and processes of reading* (4th ed., pp. 414–447). Newark, DE: International Reading Association.

Ruddell, R.B., Ruddell, M.R., & Singer, H. (Eds.). (1994). *Theoretical models and processes of reading* (4th ed.). Newark, DE: International Reading Association.

Ruddiman, J. (1997). World War II: A research/presentation project for eighth graders. *English Journal, 87*, 63–71.

Ryan, P. (1977). Warts still defy spunk water and more scientific cures. *Smithsonian, 7*, 164.

Schatz, E.K., & Baldwin, R.S. (1986). Context clues are unreliable predictors of word meaning. *Reading Research Quarterly, 21*, 439–453.

Schwartz, R.M., & Raphael, T.E. (1985). Concept of definition: A key to improving students' vocabulary. *The Reading Teacher, 39*, 198–205.

Singer, H., & Donlan, D. (1982). Active comprehension: Problem solving schema with question generation for comprehension of complex short stories. *Reading Research Quarterly, 17*, 166–186.

Smith, C.C., & Bean, T.W. (1980). The guided writing procedure: Integrating content reading and writing improvement. *Reading World, 19*, 290–294.

Stahl, S.A., & Kapinus, B.A. (1991). Possible sentences: Predicting word meanings to teach content area vocabulary. *The Reading Teacher, 45*, 36–43.

Stauffer, R.G. (1969). *Directing reading maturity as a cognitive process.* New York: Harper & Row.

Stein, H. (1978). The visual reading guide (VRG). *Social Education, 42*, 534–535.

Taba, H. (1967). *Teacher's handbook for elementary social studies.* Reading, MA: Addison-Wesley.

Tierney, R.J., & Readence, J.E. (2000). *Reading strategies and practices: A compendium* (5th ed.). Boston: Allyn & Bacon.

Tierney, R.J., & Shanahan, T. (1991). Research on the reading-writing relationship: Interactions, transactions, and outcomes. In R. Barr, M.L. Kamil, P.B. Mosenthal, & P.D. Pearson (Eds.), *Handbook of reading research: Volume II* (pp. 246–280). White Plains, NY: Longman.

Tsuchiya, Y. (1988). *Faithful elephants: A true story of animals, people and war* (T.T. Dykes, Trans.). Boston: Houghton Mifflin. (Original work published 1951)

Underwood, G., & Boot, D. (1986). Hemispheric asymmetries in developmental dyslexia: Cerebral structure or attentional strategies? *Journal of Reading Behavior, 18*, 219–228.

van Dijk, T.A. (1979). Relevance assignment in discourse comprehension. *Discourse Processes, 2*, 113–126.

van Dijk, T.A., & Kintsch, W. (1983). *Strategies of discourse comprehension.* New York: Academic Press.

Wade, S.E., & Moje, E.B. (2000). The role of text in classroom learning. In M.L. Kamil, P.B. Mosenthal, P.D. Pearson, & R. Barr (Eds.), *Handbook of reading research: Volume III.* Mahwah, NJ: Erlbaum.

Weinstein, C.E., & Mayer, R.E. (1986). The teaching of learning strategies. In M.C. Wittrock (Ed.), *Handbook of research on teaching* (3rd ed., pp. 315–327). New York: Macmillan.

Wiggins, G., & McTighe, J. (1998). *Understanding by design.* Alexandria, VA: Association for Supervision and Curriculum Development.

Wilder, M.S. (1998). Community to community: An interdisciplinary investigation for secondary students. *Science Activities, 35*, 18–23.

Index

A

FACTSTORMING, 90–91

FEATURE ANALYSIS STRATEGY, 45, 57–60, 61

FEEDBACK: guided practice and, 95–96; Possible Sentences activity and, 54, 55; and reader motivation, 7

FORECASTING PASSAGES, STRATEGIES FOR, 29–44; Anticipation Guide, 29, 31–35; Pre-Reading Plan (PReP), 29–31, 40–42; Story Impressions, 29–31, 35–37; Text Preview, 29–31, 37–39; using analogies, 29–31, 39–40; Visual Reading Guide (VRG), 29–31, 42–43. *See also* Individual strategy

FREE WRITING STRATEGY: connecting information and, 12; for writing before reading, 82–83, 84, 93–94

FREEDMAN, S., 82

FRENCH, M.P., 57–60

G

GEE, T.C., 2

GLYNN, S., 39–40

GLYNN, S.M., 70–71

GOULD, S.M., 86–87, 90

GRAPHIC ORGANIZER STRATEGY, 12, 62–64, 67–70

GRAPHICALLY REPRESENTING INFORMATION, 62–81; Graphic Organizer strategy for, 12, 62–64, 67–70; Inquiry Chart (I-Chart) strategy for, 62–64, 76–79; K-W-L strategy for, 62–64, 74–76; Outline strategy for, 62–64, 70–72; Semantic Web strategy for, 62–66, 70; Talking Drawings strategy for, 62–64, 79–81

GRAPHICS, IN TEXT, VISUAL READING GUIDE AND, 42–43

GRAVES, B.B., 1, 20–22

GRAVES, M.F., 1, 20–22, 37–39

GUIDED PRACTICE: direct instruction with writing and, 95–96; instructional cycles and, 5; Possible Sentences activity and, 54; PreReading Plan (PReP) and, 41–42; Semantic Webs and, 66; in student questioning, 22–28; Visual Reading Guide (VRG) and, 43

GUIDED WRITING PROCEDURE (GWP), 82–83, 87–90, 95

GUTHRIE, J.T., 7

H

HAAS, L.W., 86–87, 90

HAYES, D.A., 39–40

HEAD, M.H., 32–35

HEIMLICH, J.E., 57–60

HELFELDT, J.P., 25

HELLER, M., 101, 102

HENK, W.A., 25

HENNINGS, D.G., 90–92

HENNINGS SEQUENCE STRATEGY, 82–83, 90–92, 95

HOFFMAN, J.V., 76–79

HOLMES, V.L., 93

HUFFMAN, L.E., 2–3, 76

I

IDENTIFICATION WITH A STORY CHARACTER STRATEGY, 82–83, 86–87

INDEPENDENT APPLICATION, INSTRUCTIONAL CYCLES AND, 5

INFORMATION, GRAPHICALLY REPRESENTING. *See* graphically representing information

INQUIRY CHART (I-CHART) STRATEGY, FOR GRAPHICALLY REPRESENTING INFORMATION, 62–64, 76–79

INSTRUCTIONAL CYCLES, 5

INSTRUCTIONAL SCAFFOLDS, PLANNING: and factors affecting learning, 6–13; and instructional cycles, 5; and instructional time frames, 2–4. *See also* individual topic

INSTRUCTIONAL TIME FRAMES, 2–4; lesson, 4; unit, 3–4; yearly, 2–3, 4

J

JETTON, T.L., 1–2

JOHNSON, D.D., 15–16, 17

JOHNSON, M.K., 9

K

KAPINUS, B.A., 54

KNOWLEDGE BACKGROUND, OF STUDENTS: analogies strategies and, 39–40; Anticipation Guide and, 31, 32–33; categorizing words strategies and, 55–60; and connection with new ideas, 39–40; Graphic Organizer and, 68–69, 70; Inquiry Chart strategy and, 63, 78; K-W-L strategy and, 63, 74–75, 99–100; Possible Sentences activity and, 54–55; PreReading Plan (PReP) and, 40–42; Quick Writes strategy and, 94; Semantic Webs and, 66; Talking Drawings strategy and, 63, 79; Text Previews and, 38; Visual Reading Guide (VRG) and, 42–43; word map and, 72. *See also* forecasting passages

KONOPAK, B.C., 89–90

KORNFELD, J., 104

KUCAN, L., 11–12

K-W-L STRATEGY, 57, 62–64, 74–76, 99–100

L

LaBERGE, M.J., 37–39

LANGER, J.A., 40–42

LAYCOCK, S.R., 11–12

LIKERT SCALE, 58

LIST-GROUP-LABEL STRATEGY, 45, 55–57, 61

LUNSTRUM, J.P., 31

M

McCONNELL, S., 79–81

McGINLEY, W.J., 35–37

McINTOSH, M.E., 27

McKEOWN, M.G., 63

MCMURRY, F.M., 1
MCTIGHE, J., 3
MAGORIAN, M., 38
MANZO, A.V., 23–25
MAPS, UNDERSTANDING OF. *See* graphics, in text
MARINO, J.L., 86–87, 90
MARTIN, M.A., 89–90
MARTIN, S.H., 89–90
MAURER, D.W., 46
MAYER, R.E., 11–12
MEANING, OF WORDS. *See* vocabulary knowledge
MODELING: and PreReading Plan (PReP), 41–42; and student questioning, 22–23; and Visual Reading Guide (VRG), 43
MOJE, E.B., 7
MOORE, D.W., 12, 48–55, 69–70, 94–95
MOORE, S.A., 12, 48–55, 94–95
MOTIVATIONAL STRATEGIES, 6, 7–8; Free Writing and, 93; Quick Writes and, 95; and use of controversy, 31. *See also* Anticipation Guide strategy; Story Impressions strategy; Text Preview strategy
MOULTON, M.R., 93

O

OGLE, D., 74–76
OLLMAN, H.E., 93
OMANSON, R.C., 63
ORGANIZING INFORMATION: learning strategies and, 13. *See also* Data Charts; Graphic Organizer strategy; Hennings Sequence strategy; Survey Technique; Webbing
OUTLINE STRATEGY, 62–64, 70–72

P

PACE, C.M., 105–106
PALINCSAR, A.S., 23–25
PEARSON, P.D., 15–16, 17
PERSONAL/IMPERSONAL WRITING, 85
PHASE OUT/PHASE IN STRATEGIES, AND STUDENT QUESTIONING, 22–23
PHELPS, S.F., 39–40
PITTELMAN, S.D., 57–60
PLANNING PREREADING ACTIVITIES. *See* instructional scaffolds, planning
POSSIBLE SENTENCES ACTIVITY, 45, 51–55, 60–61
POSTREADING ACTIVITIES: Anticipation Guide and, 34–35; Feature Analysis strategy and, 60; K-W-L strategy and, 57; List-Group-Label strategy and, 57; Semantic Webs and, 66
PREDICTING INFORMATION: Graphic Organizer and, 69; learning strategies and, 12; Possible Sentences activity and, 51–55. *See also* Contextual Redefinition strategy; forecasting passages; Free Writing strategy; PreReading Plan (PReP); ReQuest strategy; Webbing

SEMANTIC MAPPING. *See* List-Group-Label strategy

SEMANTIC WEB STRATEGY, 62–66, 70

SHANAHAN, T., 82

SIMPSON, M.L., 31

SINGER, H., 22–23, 29

SMITH, C.C., 87–90

SOCIAL PARTICIPATION, AND READER MOTIVATION, 7

STAHL, S.A., 54

STAUFFER, R.G., 25–27

STEIN, H., 42–43

STEVENS, R., 5

STORY IMPRESSIONS STRATEGY: for forecasting passages, 29–31, 35–37; and similarities to Text Preview, 37–38

STRATEGIES FOR PREREADING QUESTIONS, 14–15; Directed Reading Activity (DRA), 14–15, 18–20; Directed Reading-Thinking Activity (DRTA), 14–15, 25–27; Question-Answer Relationships (QAR), 14–15, 17–18; ReQuest procedure, 12, 14–15, 23–25; Scaffolded Reading Experience (SRE), 14–15, 20–22; Survey Technique, 14–15, 27–28. *See also specific strategy*

STRUCTURED OVERVIEW. *See* Graphic Organizer strategy

STUDENT QUESTIONING: and active comprehension, 22–23; comprehension enhancement through, 22–28; guided practice in, 22–28; modeling and, 22–23; phase out/phase in strategies and, 22–23

STUDENT-ORIGINATED QUESTIONS, 22–28; Directed Reading-Thinking Activity (DRTA), 25–27; ReQuest strategy and, 23–25; Survey Technique and, 27–28. *See also specific strategy*

STUDENTS' BELIEFS AND OPINIONS, ANTICIPATION GUIDE AND, 32–33

SURVEY TECHNIQUE, 12, 14–15, 27–28

T

TABA, H., 56–57

TALKING DRAWINGS STRATEGY, FOR GRAPHICALLY REPRESENTING INFORMATION, 62–64, 79–81

TEACHER-ORIGINATED QUESTIONS, 16–22; Directed Reading Activity (DRA), 18–20, 23; Question-Answer Relationships (QAR) strategy, 17–18; Scaffolded Reading Experience (SRE), 20–22. *See also specific strategy*

TERMINOLOGY, OF CONTENT MATERIAL. *See* vocabulary knowledge

TEXT PREVIEW STRATEGY, 29–31, 37–39

THINKING SKILLS: critical, 76, 79; reinforcement of, 39–40

TIERNEY, R.J., 18–21, 38–39, 40–42, 67, 77, 82

TIME FRAMES, INSTRUCTIONAL. *See* instructional time frames

TSUCHIYA, Y., 36

U

UNDERSTANDING, LEVELS OF, 15–16

UNDERSTANDING VOCABULARY. *See* vocabulary knowledge

UNDERWOOD, G., 8